The
Performance
Mare

The Performance Mare

Maximizing What Your Mare Does Best

Sharon B. Smith

BOOK HOUSE

New York

Maxwell Macmillan Canada
Toronto

Maxwell Macmillan International
New York   Oxford   Singapore   Sydney

Howell Book House   Maxwell Macmillan Canada, Inc.
Macmillan Publishing Company   1200 Eglinton Avenue East
866 Third Avenue   Suite 200
New York, NY 10022   Don Mills, Ontario M3C 3N1

Macmillan Publishing Company is part of the Maxwell Communication Group of Companies.

                    Library of Congress Cataloging-in-Publication Data
          Smith, Sharon B.
              The performance mare : maximizing what your mare does best /
          Sharon B. Smith.
                  p.   cm.
              Includes bibliographical references and index.
              ISBN 0-87605-958-2
              1. Competition horses.   2. Mares.   I. Title.
          SF294.3.S48   1993
          636.1'088'8—dc20   92-41502   CIP

Macmillan books are available at special discounts for bulk purchases for sales promotions, premiums, fund-raising, or educational use. For details, contact:

                        Special Sales Director
                        Macmillan Publishing Company
                        866 Third Avenue
                        New York, NY 10022

10 9 8 7 6 5 4 3 2 1
Printed in the United States of America

Contents

Preface

IN 1874 THERE WAS LITTLE DEBATE ABOUT THE NAME OF THE MOST famous, most popular and best equine athlete in North America. It was Goldsmith Maid, the world's fastest trotter during a time when trotters drew the biggest crowds and earned the largest purses of any sporting horses. The Maid traveled coast to coast in her luxurious private railway car, competing against and usually beating all comers at each of the major tracks in the United States.

Goldsmith Maid was an extraordinary creature by anybody's standards. During her racing career, she earned $264,577, an equine earnings record that stood for almost half a century. She set the world record for the mile seven different times, five times in 1874 when she was seventeen years old. Her accomplishments inspired admiration and awe and even love. But they were not considered any more remarkable because Goldsmith Maid was female.

Why should they be? The Maid had earned the title of most famous from Flora Temple, who had lowered the world record six times. Before Flora Temple, honors went to Lady Suffolk, the first horse in the world to trot a mile in less than two and a half minutes, breaking through a long-established barrier. It was the equivalent of the human four-minute mile, and it was the thirteen-year-old gray mare Lady Suffolk who put the first hoof over the barrier.

No, it wouldn't have occurred to people who admired fine sporting horses in the nineteenth century to admire them any more or any less when they happened to be mares. Move ahead a hundred years, to 1974.

In August of that year I watched the most impressive sporting horse I've ever seen race at Saratoga. A few years before that, upon graduation from college, I'd begun a campaign to see in person as many of the great equine athletes of my time as I possibly could.

My jobs helped. First as a news reporter, then as a sports announcer, then as an equine journalist, I was able to travel the continent, watch and report on events, and visit farms, generally at somebody else's expense. I saw hundreds of good and great horses.

I saw, in action or in retirement, Secretariat and Seattle Slew, Kelso and John Henry, Jet Run and Idle Dice, Niatross and Speedy Crown. Forego bit me and I patted Alydar's neck. I watched Flatterer win a steeplechase and Ahlerich win a dressage event. But the most impressive horse I ever saw was a two-year-old filly.

To be fair, the two times I saw Secretariat in action he lost. Otherwise, my opinion might have been a little different. But he did lose, and the filly didn't. I saw her again the next year and she still didn't lose. I'm still looking for an equine athlete of any breed and either sex who can impress me more.

The filly was Ruffian. Her tragic death after a highly publicized match race has tended to overshadow her remarkable life, just as her sex has tended to confuse people's attitude toward her. Was she so good in spite of the fact that she was a filly? Was she so admired because she was female? Were her accomplishments all the more remarkable because of her sex? I pride myself on being a clear-eyed, rational observer of horses, but even I am not entirely sure if my opinion of her was colored by her sex.

In 1874 a lover of fine horses would have said that Ruffian was so good because she had the body to run fast and the determination to do it. But we know more now, and so we give Ruffian and the

Gold Medal jumper Touch of Class and the calf-roping champion Sweet And Innocent extra credit because they are female.

But do we really know more? Or have we made assumptions that bear little relationship to reality?

Try to answer these questions: Is a mare as good an athlete as a stallion or gelding? Is she worse? Could she actually be better?

Even people who seem to know everything there is to know about their horses and their sports often can't answer those questions. The organizers of Quarter Horse racing's Breeders' Classic series, faced with an overflow of entries, divided the 1991 three-year-old championship into one division for colts and one for fillies. The winning filly's trainer, the most successful conditioner in his sport's history, said afterwards that he was grateful for the split, since fillies have a better chance against their own sex.

The trainer conveniently overlooked the fact that fillies had won 75 percent of the three-year-old Classic races before the event was split up according to sex.

The correct answers to those questions are: maybe, maybe, and maybe. It depends on the sport, it depends on the mare, it depends on her training, and it depends on the attitude of the people who surround her as to whether her potential is greater, less, or just about the same as a male horse of similar quality.

But whether or not she's better or worse, she is most definitely different. An understanding and appreciation of her differences will help anybody lucky enough to own a mare get the most out of her.

You can learn to overcome the differences that work against a mare in a given sport, and you can learn to maximize the differences that make her excel. But how about the things that don't much matter, such as subtle differences in personality and character? Just enjoy them.

1

The Female
of the Species

ABOUT THE SAME TIME HUMAN BEINGS DOMESTICATED THE HORSE, they began arguing about whether stallions or mares made more useful animals. The ancient Persians preferred mares for both riding and battle. Skilled Persian breeders kept a few stallions for their stud farms, but the rest were exported to what they believed were less sophisticated kingdoms. The Sarmatians of Asia, who were greatly admired in the ancient world for the quality of their horses, knew the principle of safe gelding hundreds of years before the rest of the world figured it out. But the Sarmatians usually rode mares, too.

The Greeks were enthusiastic believers in male superiority in other aspects of life, but they were convinced that female horses were faster than males. This was important to the Greeks, who were such great fans of equine sports that racing, mounted ball games, and equine gymkhana events became an integral part of the early Olympiads. To many Greek racing fans, the four-mare chariot team was the ideal, and several famous charioteers asked in their wills that their best racing mares be buried alongside them. The historian Herodotus, sometimes called the father of history, tells us of the four-mare team of Cimon of Athens who won three Olympiads. The mares, Herodotus says, joined Cimon in a sumptuous tomb.

Many Greek soldiers also preferred mares, arguing that females were less likely to warn enemies of their approach with loud noises. Mares also, they thought, wasted less time making an elaborate process out of urinating.

But something changed with the rise of the Roman Empire. The Romans were innovative and creative horsemen. Cavalry was not originally their forte, but they developed it out of necessity and spread it through the known world as they conquered region after region. They established breeding farms throughout their empire, crossing the quick, light horse breeds of southern Asia with the stocky, cold-blooded breeds of the north. They then populated Europe with the result. Roman sportsmen raised horse racing to an art, and the average Roman citizen enjoyed horse sports even more than the Greeks had.

When the accomplished Roman horsemen concurred with the handful of early civilizations that believed the male rather than the female horse was the more useful animal, the rest of the world came to believe it too, and kept on believing for a very long time.

The Bedouin was an exception. Like the Greeks, the desert Arabs thought mares were faster than stallions and much superior as mounts in battle. They believed this so strongly that the ancestry of the traditional Arabian horse was traced through the female line, not the male. Only recently have Arabian fanciers paid much attention to sire lines. The Arab horseman admired his stallions but cherished his mares.

But the rest of the world clung to the idea that the Romans spread. Given a choice, a horseman would claim to prefer a male animal. The belief in stallion superiority—and in the superiority of geldings once the technique of castration became widespread—fit in nicely with overall societal beliefs in male superiority. Huge draft-type stallions were the favored mounts for medieval knights. Spanish soldiers, including the conquistadores who reintroduced the horse to North America, did their best to ride only stallions.

Many of the Plains Indian tribes would ride stallions to battle, feeling that anything else might be bad luck. Mares were sometimes grudgingly acknowledged to be equal or even superior to stallions in buffalo running, and the most realistic Indian horsemen must have realized that buffalo hunting tended to have more practical value than battle. But they were probably reluctant to say that aloud.

Most cultures of the past two thousand years have shared the belief that the male horse is superior to the female, particularly where the technique of gelding has allowed horsemen to eliminate some of the behavior problems of stallions. The belief has ranged from the feeling that there isn't a whole lot of difference between male and female but what difference there is benefits the male, to the thought that male horses are the only ones worth having. According to this extreme philosophy, mares are good only for bearing new horses and as ladies' mounts.

That last idea is pretty well gone; it and knighthood were in flower at the same time. Most societies believed something in between: perhaps that mares were useful but stallions and geldings made better mounts, better driving horses and better sporting animals.

People managed to maintain these ideas even when their own actions argued otherwise. Paul Revere, a courier to the Sons of Liberty in the days before the American Revolution, needed a fast horse on April 18, 1775. British troops were about to march out of the port of Boston toward Lexington and Concord, where the would-be rebels stored their arms. Revere had to make sure he could get the message to the rebels with as much notice as possible so they would be ready to defend their supplies.

The Larkin family of the Boston suburb of Charlestown was known to possess the fastest horses around. As rebel sympathizers, they willingly gave up their fastest and best. Their best was a mare of the Narragansett Pacer breed.

She turned out to be fast enough to get Revere to Lexington in time to deliver his message. Just past Lexington, Revere was stopped by British army sentries. They released him but kept the admirable Larkin mare. She was never recovered, but she remains a heroine of American history.

Eighty-five years later, on April 3, 1860, a mare kicked off the Pony Express. She carried rider Billy Richardson on a twenty-two mile leg out of St. Joseph, Missouri, completing the distance in 1 hour 45 minutes. When Richardson switched mounts, he changed to another mare. Another version of the story gives credit to rider Johnny Frey for completing the first leg of the Pony Express. No matter. In that version, Frey is also aboard a mare. In fact, most of the Pony Express horses were mares, since the company specified mares in its initial purchase order.

J. E. B. Stuart, the most famous of the Confederate cavalry generals of the Civil War, bought a horse as a gift for his commanding officer early in the conflict. Stuart picked a chestnut mare to give to Robert E. Lee. Lee named her Lucy Long, and the small, gentle animal alternated with the more famous—and male—Traveller as Lee's war horse until just a few months before Appomattox. Lee acknowledged Lucy to be Traveller's equal in war service. She had a more sensible manner and more comfortable gaits, although she was not quite as handsome as the dashing and masculine Traveller.

Lee sent her behind the lines late in 1864 to rest, then temporarily misplaced her when the Confederacy collapsed. So it was Traveller, not Lucy Long, who earned a place in history as the enduring equine symbol of the Confederacy, even though the mare had done virtually equal work. Lucy got the last laugh, though. She outlived both Lee and Traveller by nearly twenty years.

People were certainly willing to use mares, even to choose mares over male horses, in life-and-death situations. Yet those people lived in a world that tended to value male horses over female, based on some kind of presumption of superiority.

Nineteenth-century western horsemen convinced themselves that they should always pick a gelding or a well-behaved stallion for stock work, since mares were less strong. Besides, they claimed, a mare might attract wild stallions from who-knows-where. Holders of this opinion overlooked the story of the Pony Express mares, who showed neither an inclination toward weakness nor an unfortunate attraction for wild stallions.

Livery and private stable operators of the same period could read the work of James Garland, who told them in *The Private Stable* that both geldings and stallions were preferable to mares for driving purposes, although Garland failed to explain why. Perhaps he was afraid his explanation couldn't quite account for trotting mares like Lady Suffolk, Flora Temple, and Goldsmith Maid, each of whom set world records under harness well into her teens.

How could this be? How could horsemen not realize the contradiction inherent in maintaining the notion that the male horse was more useful than the female, while at the same time using and succeeding with mares?

If asked, each horseman might have claimed that the quality of his own mare was an exception. But they were rarely asked, and they probably managed to avoid dealing with the contradiction simply by refusing to think about it. Few newspaper articles of the period take any particular notice of the sex of the great nineteenth-century trotting mares, except to refer to them as "she" rather than "he." Some are even casual about that. You can find Lady Suffolk referred to as "he" in more than one newspaper article. Flora Temple did get some attention for her looks; she was described as delicate and pretty. But this was generally to contrast her with the big and rather plain Lady Suffolk, not to make a point about her sex.

Paul Revere refers to Reverend Larkin's mare as "he" in one part of his memoirs, although most historians agree that her sex was not in doubt. Revere was, apparently, either casual about his facts or concerned that he be remembered by history as a knowledgeable horseman according to the standards of the time. If this was true, he may have been more than a little hypocritical. The only horse known for sure to have been owned by Revere, a pleasure hack that he bought in 1773, was a mare.

Back to the question. How could this contradiction between belief and use exist, particularly as people became more educated and supposedly more willing to look at the real world rather than the presumed world? In part, it's because we *do* know something about zoology and biology.

People have known since very early times that males and females of most animal species are different from one another, and the differences are not just in their reproductive organs. People knew this from simple observation long before the science of anatomy confirmed it.

The physical difference between the sexes is called *sexual dimorphism*, and it exists in almost every species. In some, the difference is so profound that the male and female look like they are members of separate species. Compare a gaudy, crested male wood duck to his smaller, plain brown mate. Unless you are a serious bird watcher, you might assume that you're watching an odd, interspecies relationship. Most other species of duck show a similar sexual variation.

Yet in other species of birds male and female are nearly identical. Until recently, only an operation done by a veterinarian could expose the difference between male and female in many species of parrots. But that is an exception. The majority of warmblooded creatures show some obvious sexual dimorphism.

People with a modest knowledge of a particular species can usually tell the difference between sexes. This is because the most common difference between male and female is size.

Although there are plenty of individual variations, you can safely say that, within a species and within a breed of that species, most males are bigger than most females. The size differences vary tremendously. There is a fraction of an ounce difference between male and female chickadees. But a bull elephant seal may outweigh his mate by nearly a ton.

But the assumption is one we can and do make: male is bigger than female. We see it all around us. Moreover, we also assume that the bigger male is also the stronger of the two. In most cases, this assumption is accurate.

But there are exceptions. In some breeds of rabbit, in several species of bat, and in many possums, females are a little larger than males. In whales, the difference is more substantial. The female blue whale is the biggest animal on earth, ranging from 70 to 110 feet in length in adulthood. The male blue whale is much smaller, although comparative figures are hard to come by. Records, most of which date from whaling days, concentrate on extra-large females.

We should pay special attention to one other exception to the rule of male-is-bigger: the predatory birds. In almost all of the raptors, the female is significantly bigger than her mate. Like the whale, the female raptor is more than a little bigger. Among many falcons and hawks, the female is a full one-third larger than the male. She is stronger, usually faster, and able to hunt bigger prey. The males may be a bit more agile and able to catch small quick mammals, but the female is the more powerful hunter and brings home the biggest meals to the nest.

The female is also the bird of choice in the sport of falconry. The fastest of the sport hunting birds is the female prairie falcon, followed by the stronger and nearly as fast female gyrfalcon and the powerful female peregrine falcon. It may be no coincidence that a modern center of falconry is in Saudi Arabia and the neighboring Arab emirates, where female horses are also considered faster and sturdier.

In spite of what falconry might tell us about the dangers of making blanket assumptions about athletic ability based on sex, we maintain our belief that males, being larger and stronger than females, make better athletes, at least in open competition where strength and speed count. We do this because we see the truth of the belief among the animals closest to us: the higher primates, including homo sapiens.

But even within the primates, there is great variation in sexual dimorphism. The 400-pound male gorilla is twice as heavy as the female. The same ratio is true of the orangutan, although the male of that species averages only 200 pounds. But consider these figures from the two primate species that are most similar genetically to human beings. On average, the chimpanzee male is only slightly larger than the female—a matter of a couple of inches and few pounds. The male and female bonobo have the *same* average height, 3 feet 9 inches, although the average male weighs nearly 30 percent more.

Since we don't use nonhuman primates for sporting purposes, these figures are nothing more than intriguing snippets of scientific trivia. They tell us nothing about comparative athletic abilities of male and female. For that, we have to look at the highest of the primates.

Female human athletes have improved dramatically during the second half of the twentieth century. Partly because the women's movement helped redefine femininity, partly because of increased cultural emphasis on leisure for everyone, and partly because of an economic reality that made women's athletics profitable, women athletes play an increasingly important role in the sporting world. Female records have improved faster than male records. Running times, swimming times, jumping heights and throwing distances show greater increases for women than for men. But this doesn't mean that any change is occurring in the physical nature of women and men.

Studies suggest that untrained females have about 50 percent of the *strength* of untrained males, although the world-wide average for male *size* superiority is somewhat less than 20 percent. The strength differential is not entirely a result of genetics, since boys are encouraged from a very early age to run and throw and wrestle.

The more legitimate comparison is between highly trained members of each sex. The studies don't agree here, but they all say that the gap narrows dramatically with training. A 1948 study reported in *Research Quarterly* by Carrie Belle Morris showed trained women athletes to have 78 percent of the strength of trained men. Dr. Jack Wilmore, who studied women athletes at the University of California in the 1970s, reported the difference to be 10 percent. He said that he believed that trained women will eventually have 95 percent the strength of men.

The rate of improvement has led some researchers to claim that the gap will eventually be narrowed to nothing in a few sports. UCLA scientists raised a storm of comment in 1992 when they claimed, based on an examination of world records, that women marathon runners would be running the event as fast as men by the turn of the twenty-first century. Other scientists say the laws of nature will eventually prevail, claiming that women runners will improve up to the physical capacity of the female of the species, and then the improvement rate will just parallel that of men, so the men will never be surpassed.

Women are different from men in ways that affect athletic performance—ways that training cannot change, no matter how hard the female athlete works. There is considerable variation among individuals, but here are the general facts. The average woman has narrower shoulders than the average man, as well as a lower center of gravity, and different angles in the arm and pelvis. She has a higher fat-to-muscle ratio, a physical characteristic that helps her with childbearing. She is somewhat shorter, with proportionally shorter arms and legs. The fat-to-muscle ratio, the shoulder difference, and the different center of gravity gives most men greater upper body strength than most women.

Yes, women are different from men. The difference usually gives men a comparative advantage, but it occasionally leads to superior female performance in some sports. Women's names predominate in any listing of extraordinary accomplishments in outdoor long-distance swimming, for example. Extra fat is an advantage in this sport, both for insulation and energy.

In 1926 Gertrude Ederle made the fastest crossing of the English Channel, when she swam the distance in 14 hours 31 minutes. In 1977 Cindy Nicholas made a round-trip crossing in 19 hours 55 minutes, an extraordinary time.

In the equine sports, women riders may have an advantage, or they may not. Women jockeys have not been able to make as great an impact on the racing sports as some observers thought they were going to do when the opportunity breakthrough occurred in the late 1960s. Only Thoroughbred jockey Julie Krone could be considered to be riding fully on a par with men as the 1990s began. In 1992 she won the riding title at Belmont Park, where competition between jockeys is intense. But in dressage, endurance riding and probably show jumping, women appear to be fully equal, if not superior.

Although we should never make assumptions based only on levels of participation or success—those can be affected by opportunity—we can draw some conclusions about human biology and riding. In spite of what certain heavyweight riders might like to believe, horses perform better carrying lighter weights. In the equine sports where weight is usually not regulated, including most jumping and dressage, women riders can benefit from their average lower weight.

Some competitions in these sports do require minimum weights, but these weights are often so light that heavier riders still have a disadvantage.

In sports where weight is strictly regulated and assigned, usually the racing sports, women have no advantage, since the horse carries an assigned weight. As luck would have it, riders in most of the racing sports also benefit dramatically from upper body strength, in which the average woman is much inferior to the average man. The woman jockey may find it easier to make weights than the male jockey, but that is her only biological advantage.

Upper body strength can certainly help in the nonracing sports, but it is not quite as important as it is in flat racing. The Julie Krones of the world aside, women jockeys have not had as great an impact in the upper levels of racing as female riders have had in other horse sports. Since racing is the most publicized and highest paying of the equine sports, this fact has reinforced the belief— even among horse people—that female athletes are not fully equal to men.

That may be a key to the centuries of conflicting assumptions about the comparative value of male and female horses for both utility and sport. Males are bigger, males are stronger and males perform better. People observe that in most animals and in themselves.

But how accurate is such an observation in terms of horses? As it turns out, the answer is not entirely clear. We know that male horses tend to be somewhat larger than female horses of similar genetic background. The words to note are "tend," "somewhat," and "similar." There are differences, but the differences are not always obvious to casual observers. Moreover, the sexual dimorphism of horses is not the same as for humans. See Chapter 2 for more information on physical differences between male and female horses and the effects those differences may have in performance. Chapter 3 discusses psychological differences, which most experts do not consider part of sexual dimorphism. Read these chapters and decide for yourself.

In the meantime, accept this fact: There are differences between male and female horses which may or may not account for one of the equine world's ongoing mysteries. Why is it that fillies and mares who can compete effectively against male horses in some sports are noticeably uncompetitive in others, and are demonstrably superior in still others?

A few years ago, the pony string of the top American polo team consisted of twenty-three mares and one old gelding. The gelding was given little playing time, but the trainer was fond of him and used him as a mount during training sessions. Other high-goal polo teams are also heavily weighted in favor of mares, although many do use a few geldings, too.

Contrast this with steeplechasing, where a recent year of timber, point-to-point, and steeplechase racing in the United States saw mares win only about 3 percent of the recognized races. The percentage of mares in top-level dressage competition and in three-day eventing is almost as low.

There are mysterious and—at first glance—inexplicable contrasts within individual equine sports, too. Harness racing consists of competition at the trot and the pace. Trotting fillies and mares, although they usually race in same-sex events these days, would probably be fully competitive with male horses if they competed regularly with them. They certainly were in the past. Pacing females, on the other hand, are measurably slower than colts and geldings. North American pacers and trotters are members of the same breed—the Standardbred. The same drivers are in the sulkies for both kinds of racing. Most trainers have both trotters and pacers in their stables. The equipment is similar. So why the differences in female performance?

Among flat racers there is a similar contrast. A female entrant in Thoroughbred racing's Kentucky Derby or Epsom Derby is very rare indeed. But a filly in Quarter Horse racing's premier event, the All-American Futurity, is a common sight. Fillies often comprise half the field in that multimillion-dollar race. In recent years, with the growth of same-sex events in Quarter Horse racing, fewer fillies win the big races, but in the past fillies won at least half of the big-money races, sometimes more. Breed alone doesn't pro-

Can you identify the mares among these three horses waiting for a western pleasure class? Sexual dimorphism in the horse is less significant than it is in any other species, making quick identification difficult. (The mares are left and center.)

This Welsh Pony hunter mare is fully competitive with the geldings on her circuit, possibly because she is not noticeably "feminine" in type.

vide the entire explanation, since the modern racing Quarter Horse is the product of an open stud book that makes her at least three-quarters and more likely fifteen-sixteenths Thoroughbred. In the nonracing western events, you will see some mares in roping, many mares in bull dogging, and occasionally a majority of mares in cutting competitions.

In other equine sports, you find similar hard-to-explain situations. There is little doubt that Grand Prix–level show jumpers are mostly male. Yet for the half century that coincided with the burgeoning interest in show jumping, only two horses won double gold medals for jumping in the Olympics. Both were mares—the German crossbred Halla in 1956 and the American Thoroughbred Touch of Class in 1984. Each differed considerably in conformation from the ideal Grand Prix jumper of the period, and each was clearly as good as male horses who looked the way conventional wisdom said they should. Yet neither caused riders and trainers to acquire mares in greater numbers. In the last few years, though, international show jumping has seen a slight increase in the use of mares, particularly by German riders.

Female success in sports that involve subjective judgment is harder to fathom. There are few successful mares at the highest levels of international dressage, even though most horse people will tell you that mares are sensitive and many are highly intelligent and quick learners. The 1992 World Cup dressage finals showed a typical ratio of male to female. The finals consisted of eleven stallions or geldings and one mare. But think about this: The lone mare won everything, including the Grand Prix, the freestyle and the overall World Cup title.

Some Saddlebred and Morgan people spend their careers trying to decide whether they are better or worse off going to major competitions with a mare. The in-hand single-sex divisions are easy enough to figure out, but a mare's showing in a pleasure or Grand Champion competition often depends less on her rivals than on her breed and the tastes of the judge of the particular class.

So there it is. Mares are sometimes better, sometimes worse and sometimes just about the same as stallions and geldings. Why?

In part the answer undoubtedly has to do with physical characteristics, as we will see in future chapters. The few physical differences that exist between male and female in the equine species work to a mare's advantage in some sports and to her disadvantage in others.

There are mental differences, too. Some are hormonal, and these tend to hurt rather than help. But they don't hurt as much as even experienced horse people sometimes think. Some mental differences appear to be the result of deep-seated characteristics that domestication has failed to remove from the genetic inheritance of what used to be a wild animal. See Chapter 3 for information on the mind of the mare.

The differing performance levels of mares in a variety of sports may be accounted for in large part by the unconscious prejudices of the human beings who train and handle them. If less is demanded of a mare, less will come from her. On the other hand, her differences do sometimes require slightly different handling. For example, a mare in heat will require more care and attention.

What is important is this: Females differ from males in horses as they do in every other species of bird and mammal. But the difference is not the same as it is in other species. Assuming that it is can lead to inefficient and ineffective use of a valuable resource.

If you have assumptions about mares, you are to be forgiven. Horse people have the weight of several thousand years of assumptions to deal with. Just try to forget them and look at the female horse for what she is, not what other people think she should be.

2

The Physical Mare

THERE ARE FEW SPECIES ON EARTH MORE MANIPULATED BY MAN THAN the horse. Even the search for the perfect Pomeranian or the classic Collie has failed to change the reality that pet dogs often choose their own mates, usually without their owners' permission. The breeding of livestock is somewhat more controlled, but only at the most sophisticated levels of farming do the owners of cattle, sheep and swine worry about much beyond getting their animals pregnant.

Horses are different. With the exception of scattered herds of feral horses around the world—and excepting the colt who can jump a higher fence than anybody thought he could—horses do not usually reproduce unless their owners intend them to. Those owners are generally looking for something more than a 90-pound warm body eleven months down the line. They want something that can run, or that can pull weight, or that can jump. So they select their breeding stock accordingly.

They choose the fastest stallion they can find within their price range for a stud fee. Or they buy a mare with the kind of neck and shoulders they admire in a driving horse. Would-be breeders of jumpers try to choose a stallion with a proven ability to jump over something higher than his shadow and breed him to a mare whose conformation suggests she might foal a jumper.

For thousands of years, people have been selecting their equine breeding stock for specific physical characteristics and the performance that goes along with them. What this has done is to make it very difficult to identify characteristics that are inherent in the species and those that have been bred into horses through all those centuries of manipulation.

Differences between male and female horses are among the characteristics that may have been altered by selective breeding. Here is an illustration that may or may not be true. Suppose that 2,000 years ago mares were as much smaller than stallions as women are than men—with the female just 70 to 80 percent of the male size. Horse owners would understand quickly that if they wanted to utilize horses to provide meat, haul equipment or carry soldiers into battle, the large horse was probably more useful than the small one. So they would tend to select only their largest and strongest mares to breed. The result would be larger horses in general, but it may also have been larger mares in particular.

Many seemingly unrelated physical characteristics of horses often appear to be sex-connected. For example, the best and most breedable female members of a particular female family may be almost uniformly bay, and uniformly good at running or jumping. The male horses from the family may be less consistent in their colors and less likely to share the family talents. On the other hand, the males of the family may be the ones to show consistent characteristics. The same can be true of sire lines. This means that people may have bred for larger horses and may have seen to it that they got larger mares.

Since few statistics were kept in the early days of planned horse breeding, we will never know if the relative size of male and female horses has changed from the time when the horse was exclusively wild and selected its own mates. In fact, you might be able to argue that the difference between the sexes has increased. You could claim that breeders would pick a small, feminine mare to breed, assuming she would be more fertile and more motherly. It's not likely, but it's possible.

We simply do not know for sure, but we do know that human intervention has caused both considerable change in the conformational characteristics of the modern horse and tremendous variation among breeds. Human intervention has also created what is essentially a third sex in the equine species, and this also has to be considered when trying to determine and then to deal with the physical differences between male and female horses.

Castration causes changes in every animal that undergoes the process, but the number and significance of the changes vary from species to species. A dog owner notices little change in a neutered male. The neutered Rover may be less inclined to roam the neighborhood in search of an appealing bitch, and he may be somewhat less aggressive, but Rover will not behave or look much different from his unneutered littermate Spike, if Rover and Spike were similar dogs to begin with.

At the other extreme, cattle undergo dramatic physical as well as behavioral changes upon castration. If not sent to market at a young age, a castrated male steer becomes huge and sluggish. Think of an enormous draft ox when you want to picture a neutered male bovine.

Horses fit somewhere between dogs and cattle, undergoing measurable change upon castration but not becoming dramatically different creatures. We're talking about male horses here. While it *is* possible to spay a female horse—removing her uterus, her ovaries or both—the procedure is almost never done to improve the performance potential or disposition of a filly or mare. Abdominal surgery on a large animal is far too difficult, expensive and dangerous for that. With horses, spaying is sometimes performed to provide safe "teaser" mares for artificial insemination and occasionally on recipient mares for embryo transfer, but in each case the mares receive hormones to make up for the supply they have lost, negating any effect the operation might have on their physical or mental states.

But castrating a male horse is safe, quick and inexpensive. It is the rule rather than the exception among performance horses because stallions are often difficult and dangerous to train and handle. This means that when we compare female horses to male, we have to compare them twice—once to stallions and once to geldings.

Keep that in mind as we explore the big question: how *do* mares differ physically from stallions and geldings? There is plenty of observational data but little in the way of controlled, multibreed studies. The general belief is that the sexual dimorphism of horses is less than many horse people assume.

We should know more than we do. You would think that breeders and veterinary researchers would want to find out everything there is to know about the horse, since the most valuable individual animals on the face of the earth are horses. The Thoroughbred stallion Alydar reached a total value of nearly $120 million in the early 1980s, based on his per-share price of nearly $3 million. The mare Miss Oceana was sold at auction for $7 million in 1985, even though she had never borne a foal and could reasonably expect, at best, only seven or eight foals in her lifetime. (She didn't even get that. She died foaling a couple of years later.)

Horse markets have sunk to more realistic levels since the 1980s. Today they are based more on performance possibilities than on breeding potential. Even so, dozens of untried yearlings and unbroken young horses of various breeds are each sold for more than half a million dollars every single year. In some of the high-priced breeds, you are likely to spend more on a filly than a colt. That will probably happen at a Quarter Horse auction. At a Standardbred auction, the highest-priced individual may be of either sex. At a major Thoroughbred auction, the sales topper will almost certainly be a colt, but there will be no shortage of expensive fillies. If you are buying a top-level dressage prospect or one bred for Grand Prix show jumping, expect to pay far more for a young colt or a gelding than you will for a filly.

Clearly it is about time that we had some hard data to back up, clarify or change what we think we know about the comparative differences in conformation and performance potential of male and female horses. Fortunately, both veterinary researchers and lay analysts agree. Most of the ongoing research involves young, growing horses, and the discoveries about sex differences are secondary to the information being developed on the effects on a horse's size that results from the month of foaling, feeding, age of dam and so on. Nevertheless, the research does provide us with information on sexual dimorphism in the horse and allows us to compare what we assume with what is fact. Here is what we know.

Body Temperature

For reasons that are not entirely clear, female horses usually have higher average body temperatures than male horses, even allowing for variations due to season, time of day, age and other factors that affect animals' temperatures. The difference does not seem very great: 100°F for a mare and 99.7°F for a stallion. But it is large enough and consistent enough that at least one widely used veterinary table of temperatures for domestic animals includes single listings for cattle, cats, cows, dogs, sheep, pigs and so on. The horse gets two: one for male and one for female. Ovulation may account for this variation in body temperature.

Does this odd little variation have any effect on the performance potential of the two sexes? Unfortunately, there has been little research on the question. Could it mean that a mare may suffer more on a hot day than does a stallion or gelding? On the other hand, could it mean that she can perform better than an otherwise equal male in extremely cold weather?

There is some empirical evidence to answer that last question in the affirmative. Thoroughbred trainers at New York's Aqueduct racetrack have known for a couple of decades—ever since year-round racing was introduced—that mares seem to thrive in temperatures that could freeze the noses off their jockeys. Many run their fastest races of the year during January and February. Fat protection plays no role here, as it might in female humans, since the trainers are dealing with thin, fit racehorses who have little fat regardless of sex. The absence of distracting estrus periods could be a factor in the blooming of race mares in winter, but maybe

Almost all horses are more comfortable in cold weather than humans are, but a slightly higher body temperature may make mares appreciate the cold even more.

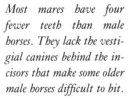

Most mares have four fewer teeth than male horses. They lack the vestigial canines behind the incisors that make some older male horses difficult to bit.

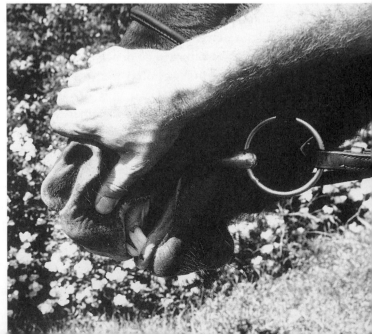

an internal furnace that burns just a little hotter is helping them too.

Almost all horses are comfortable in colder weather than their owners think possible, but it may be that mares are even more comfortable. Experiment with your own mare. Warm her up properly, of course. Then work her in your usual way. You may discover that she is more attentive, learns better and enjoys her lessons more in winter. Unfortunately, the same probably cannot be said of you.

Teeth

Male and female horses usually have different numbers of teeth. There are exceptions: males with so-called "female" mouths and vice versa. But the exceptions are rare. Each sex has thirty-six essential teeth, with the upper and lower jaw each containing six incisors to cut and grasp food and twelve molars to grind it before swallowing.

Many horses, male and female, also have so-called wolf teeth just in front of the molars. When present, they usually appear in the upper jaw, although very occasionally a lower jaw will include one or more. There seems to be no pattern as to whether wolf teeth are more common in male or female horses. Many veterinarians and equine dentists recommend the removal of wolf teeth because they can interfere with the bit. The removal, which is often done before a bit is ever inserted into a horse's mouth, is usually simple, since wolf teeth have shallow roots. Wolf teeth that cause no problem with the bit are sometimes left in. Consult your vet or equine dentist if your filly has wolf teeth.

You will probably not have to consult your vet about the other odd set of teeth that nature inflicted upon the modern horse. These are the four vestigial canines, called tushes, located just behind the incisors, two in each jaw. Most male horses have them and most females either lack them or have only very tiny ones. They are not so easy to remove, and the mare retains a dental advantage throughout her life because of the absence of tushes.

Nature probably provided the prehistoric stallion with sharp canines to help him protect himself and his harem of mares from predators. But they are nothing but a burden to the modern stallion and gelding. As the horse ages, tushes become longer and sharper, often making bit insertion difficult. If they grow outward, they can irritate the skin of the mouth. They also, in the mouth of a stallion or grouchy gelding, can endanger other horses and people. It hurts enough being bitten by a set of flat incisors. Imagine what a sharp canine can do to the skin.

So owners of male horses must make sure the vet or the dentist pays extra attention to the canines when it comes time to float the teeth. Owners of mares should also make sure that they or anybody else who owns a gelding turned out with their mares pays attention to canine care. Otherwise, a playful nip in the paddock can turn into a serious gash.

The lack of tushes may or may not mean that a mare has the potential to be more responsive to the bit, since a bit may, even if well fitted, slide forward to make contact with the canines and distract or annoy the horse. We have only observation to rely on, but many horse people do believe that mares tend to be softer-mouthed than geldings or stallions.

It is true that, with the possible exception of dressage, mares often excel in sports where mouth responsiveness is important. This may be a result of treatment. Consciously or otherwise, riders may take extra care with a filly's mouth during training, assuming she is a more delicate creature. But the lack of canines may play a role too.

Internal Differences

As in almost all mammals, the mare's reproductive organs are internal, while the stallion's are external. Although this fact does not dramatically change her physiology, it does have some effect on her conformation—as we will see later—as well as on her other internal organs. Unfortunately for her, the effect is not particularly good.

Colic, the biggest killer of adult horses, is more common in female than male horses. Mares account for as much as three-quarters of large colon torsion, or twisting, which is perhaps the deadliest form of colic. Half the victims of twisted intestine and colon blockage are post-foaling mares, and displacement caused by the foaling process is undoubtedly part of the cause. But expectant mares also fall victim in higher than normal percentages. Other torsion victims are evenly divided between males and nonpregnant females.

Mare owners can't do much about facts of anatomy that affect the digestive system, but they can make sure that their mares, in foal or not, get adequate exercise, sufficient roughage and plenty of water. Owners may be inclined to pamper a mare, particularly one who is in foal or who has recently foaled. But giving her extra stall rest and more concentrated feed than she needs may be risking her life rather than helping her.

Height and Weight

Mares are somewhat shorter and somewhat lighter than males of similar breeding, but the difference is not as great as it is in many other species. Weight is seldom recorded for horses, since few owners have access to livestock scales. A horse's actual weight—as opposed to fat levels—only matters when animals are sold by the pound. But even in the case of more valuable horses, weight is becoming more important as trainers realize that weight changes reflect condition. English trainers have led the way in this area, but horse people around the world are now gradually becoming more willing to invest in and use livestock scales.

This trend may give us better statistics on equine weight patterns. For now, most recorded horse weights are merely educated guesses. The most widely used statistics are those compiled by D. P. Willoughby in 1975. These figures, the ones currently used by veterinary researchers in their growth and nutrition studies, suggest that the average stallion weighs about 10 percent more than the average mare of similar breeding and type.

We should have better statistics on horse heights, since height is one of the characteristics used to identify the individual horse. Moreover, a height measuring stick is considerably cheaper than a livestock scale. Up to a point, this is true. A breed registry can give you an average range for its members, but the range will be rather generous. But even if you had the ability to record and then average heights according to sex for a large enough sampling of the breed for statistical validity, the results would still be misleading. Your figures would represent the result of decades or even centuries of human intervention.

Still, height statistics remain easier to obtain than weight statistics for a large number of horses, so we might expect a height comparison between male and female to be more accurate. The Willoughby statistics referred to earlier tell us that the average stallion is less than 1 percent taller than the average mare. Most horse people believe that to be a negligible difference—just over half an inch in a 16-hand 2-inch horse.

It comes down to this: Male horses are taller and weigh more than females, although the difference in weight is greater than the difference in height. In both categories, the difference is much less than in the human species.

Interestingly, geldings may end up taller than they would have if they had been left entire. As sexual maturity approaches—at about eighteen months to two years for male horses—testosterone causes a quick closure in the growth plates of the long bones. If a horse is gelded before that testosterone influx, puberty becomes a slower process, sometimes allowing bone growth to last longer than it does for an uncastrated male. But he does not necessarily acquire greater weight along with his greater height. Mature stallions are usually the heaviest of fit horses, since their regular influx of testosterone gives them more muscle than either mares or geldings of similar breeding.

Bone Size

Projects involving newborn and growing foals have uncovered another physical difference between male and female. Quarter Horse and Thoroughbred studies show that males are born with more substantial bone and maintain this advantage until puberty. The difference is consistent and probably continues through life. A University of Georgia study conducted between 1984 and 1987 shows that at birth colts have a cannon bone circumference about 4 percent larger than fillies. The difference was maintained through their yearling year, which was when the study ended. A study jointly conducted by Cornell University and Windfields Farm of Canada of nearly 2,000 foals showed similar results in the 1970s, with the difference continuing through puberty and probably adulthood. Other studies suggest about a 6 percent cannon bone advantage to male horses.

This cannon bone difference is greater than the average height difference but less than the weight difference between male and female. It suggests that heavier skeletal structure as well as heavier muscling contribute to the greater weight of the male.

It's highly unclear whether this affects performance or soundness. A Cornell University study of breakdowns at New York racetracks in the 1980s found that fillies and mares are no more or less likely to suffer fractures during races than colts, geldings and stallions.

Body Structure

Male and female horses from a similar genetic background are likely to have structural differences. The differences are slight, but the educated eye can see them. Occasionally, the tapemeasure can verify them. The differences can affect a horse's ability to excel in various sports.

Hindquarters

Female horses are usually wider in the hindquarters than male horses of the same breed and type. This may be nature's why of providing adequate room for a growing foal. The difference between the sexes is not enormous—not nearly as noticeable as between the hips of men and women, for example. In fact, there is greater hindquarter variation between the breeds than between the sexes within the same breed. A stock-type Quarter Horse gelding will be much broader in the beam than a Thoroughbred mare bred for distance. But if you compare each of those horses to an opposite-sex full or half sibling of similar type, you will probably find the female to be a little wider behind. Hindquarter structure does not seem to be affected by castration.

The mare may also be somewhat more inclined to have higher hindquarters than withers. This is often considered a conformation flaw, but many outstanding performers—many of them mares—share this characteristic.

Neck

Female horses are almost always narrower and sometimes shorter in the neck than male horses, particularly stallions. In some breeds, stallions develop extremely thick necks or noticeable crests, or both. Such necks can add as much as 200 pounds to a stallion's forequarters, thereby drastically limiting his agility and affecting his center of gravity. The stallion is most likely to put on weight in the neck during the breeding season, when his body produces greater amounts of testosterone. Whether or not thick necks are unsightly is a matter of opinion, but there is no doubt that they affect balance.

Geldings who are castrated after maturity retain much of the extra neck weight. Castration earlier can keep the neck thinner, but geldings usually have slightly thicker necks than mares of similar breeding. Weight in the neck is believed to be an advantage in jumping, since the downward propulsion of the front of the body

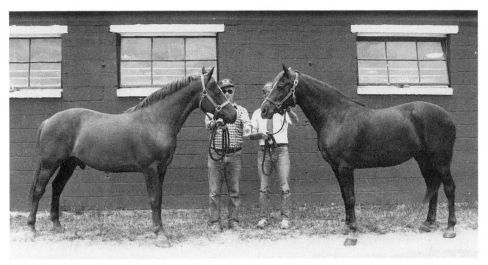

The University of Connecticut's full brother and sister seven-year-old Morgans, UC WildeMark and UC Holiday were foaled the same month, thanks to embryo transfer. Mark (left) has the heavier neck and bone of the male horse, while Holiday has a lighter neck, slightly less bone and good round hindquarters, typical of the mare.

Mares tend to be wider in the hindquarters than male horses of similar breed and type.

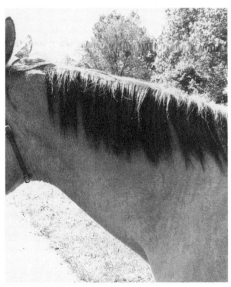

Even a bulldog-type Quarter Horse mare has a finer neck than a similar male horse would be likely to possess.

after it clears the obstacle helps lift the rest of the body over the jump.

The comparatively lighter neck on female horses may help explain why they seem to have some protection from two serious afflictions of many performance horse breeds. Thoroughbreds, and to a slightly lesser extent Quarter Horses, Morgans and other breeds, suffer in significant numbers from wobbler syndrome. The condition occurs when malformation, injury or disease damages the spine, destroying coordination. Three times as many males as females develop wobbler syndrome.

Tall, long-necked horses also suffer more roaring, a condition in which paralysis of a vocal cord constricts the airway. It is extremely common in male Thoroughbreds, and in male horses with substantial Thoroughbred blood. Mares do become roarers, particularly Thoroughbred-type mares with long necks, but it is possible that their slightly lesser height and substantially lesser weight up front help protect some of them from the condition. Some veterinary researchers are convinced that both roaring and wobbler syndrome have genetic origins and that the genes can be inherited by either sex. But physical differences between the sexes in front may give protection to mares.

Some horse people think that mares are also more likely to be a little longer in the body in comparison to height than similarly bred male horses. This belief is based on informal observation rather than scientific study, but if it's true, it would help explain the talents of mares in trotting, in which a long barrel lessens the chance of opposite leg interference.

In 1903 the tiny chestnut mare Lou Dillon became the first horse of either sex to trot a mile in less than two minutes. She was extraordinarily long-bodied in comparison to her height. She measured a full 5 inches more from breast to hindquarters than she did from the ground to the top of her rump. (No withers height is recorded for Lou Dillon, but it was probably the same or possibly somewhat lower than her rump height, making her long body even more remarkable.) Compare her measurements to those of the gelding Greyhound, who became the dominant trotter in the world thirty years later. Greyhound was a full hand taller at the withers than he was long.

Head

Among the secondary sex characteristics that appear in mature stallions is a wide, heavy jaw. The increase in jaw size varies from individual to individual, but it can lead to a bitting and control problem in some male horses. As with the neck, the extent of the characteristic in geldings can depend on the age at castration.

Manipulating Size and Conformation

Is it possible to alter the size or physical characteristics of a filly or mare if you want her to compete in a sport that seems to favor heavy male horses? You can try. But you may do more harm than good. Besides, there is no compelling evidence that any changes that do occur will make your mare any stronger, impel her to run faster or encourage her to jump higher. There is also conflicting evidence as to whether either of the two primary methods of altering growth patterns actually do much to affect the ultimate size of a mare.

Feed

The feed that goes into a mare certainly affects her weight and bone health, and the feed that went into her as a young, growing filly certainly affected the skeletal size she now possesses as an adult. This does not mean that there is a direct, progressive relationship between size and feed. Feed and nonpharmacological nutritional supplements will not allow a mare or any horse to grow beyond its genetic capacity for size, with one exception. If she is fed more calories than she burns up, she will add body fat, although the capacity for body fat also seems to be limited genetically.

What careful attention to feed can do is see to it that a filly grows to her capacity and that a mare maintains muscle and bone density. That seems simple, but in practice it's more complex. Each of the nutrients that plays a role in size is potentially dangerous if not fed or supplemented properly.

Protein

Protein is the primary nutritional contributor to muscle development. The past few years have seen changing scientific opinion about protein requirements in the horse and about the potential danger of overfeeding. The news is mostly good. Horses appear to need less than previously thought. You will see why this is good news when you price lower-protein feeds in comparison to high-protein mixes. Growing fillies, as well as pregnant and lactating mares, need more than adult horses.

The National Research Council, which establishes nutritional guidelines for people and animals, points out that protein requirements are based on body size, not level of activity. The hard-working mare and the more lightly used one require essentially the same percentage, but the more active mare will receive more in total volume, since she needs more feed in general. Feeding a higher percentage of protein appears to be of no benefit to either her muscles or her health, and there is ongoing debate as to whether feeding excess protein will harm more than your pocketbook. In humans, excess protein has been linked to kidney disease and other serious problems. A study conducted by two prominent Cornell University veterinarians suggests that overfeeding in general—and the overfeeding of protein in particular—can contribute to skeletal damage in growing horses.

There is no universal agreement on the potential dangers of excess protein, but until there is evidence that extra protein provides any extra benefit, there seems to be little reason to overfeed. Consult your vet, a nutritional specialist or one of the recommended general horse care books in the appendix.

Calcium, Phosphorus and Vitamin D

Calcium, phosphorus and vitamin D all work together to form and maintain bone, so the temptation to supplement for them is great. Care must be taken with each.

Vitamin D usually needs supplementation only in horses who spend virtually all their time indoors. Sunlight provides all that most horses require. Oversupplementation is a danger, because vitamin D is stored within the body rather than excreted. That makes it easier for the vitamin to reach toxic levels in the horse's body. Ironically, among the problems caused by vitamin D toxicity is bone damage.

Calcium and phosphorus must both be present for bone growth and maintenance, and they must be in balance. The most recent research tells us that phosphorus should never exceed calcium in the diet. So at worst, a 1:1 ratio between calcium and phosphorus should be maintained. An adult horse can handle a ratio of 3:1 or even 4:1, but a growing horse has much less ability to excrete extra calcium.

In addition to the ratio, the volume of calcium and phosphorus must be considered. Excess and improperly balanced calcium and phosphorus can contribute to skeletal problems, so this is definitely not a "more is better" area. The goal in feeding these nutrients should be to provide enough for optimum bone health without overdoing it.

Feed stores usually have a supply of booklets and other information on the content of commercial horse feeds, and they or your local cooperative extension office can give you an analysis of the locally available hay and grain. Commercial feeds will almost always have the proper balance as well as sufficient quantities of nutrients, and you will have problems only if you feel you must supplement.

Again, consult your veterinarian or an equine nutritionist if you have questions.

Anabolic Steroids

Anabolic steroids, laboratory-produced male hormones, have an important role to play in the care of sick or stressed horses. They help prevent the loss of muscle tissue in postsurgical horses, horses who cannot eat properly because of illness or old age and horses who are stall bound because of injury. But some veterinarians and horse owners have experimented with them on healthy horses in an effort to improve performance. Some people who have used them on healthy horses insist they can see improvement in ability, although no major scientific study has been able to verify this.

Anabolic steroids—two have been approved for use in horses, boldenone undecylenate and stanozolol—are similar to testosterone, the hormone that gives males their secondary sex characteristics. In horses, these include the stallion's heavy neck and extra muscle size, as well as his aggressive behavior. Although few owners of mares want the neck, they do sometimes like the idea of more muscle and a little more aggression in their mares.

Studies at the University of Pennsylvania and Colorado State confirm that owners who give their mares steroids—particularly boldenone undecylenate—certainly get the extra aggression. Some mares show dramatic stallionlike behavior, including fighting and mounting other horses. A Texas A&M study finds no increase in size for a group of steroid-treated mares. The Colorado State steroid mares actually lost weight, probably because they expended so much energy in their aggression against each other.

Virtually every study done on anabolic steroids reports reproductive problems in some horses who have been treated with them, boldenone in particular. Many mares don't come into season properly, don't show estrus or refuse to be bred. Some even suffer ovarian damage. The other steroid—stanozolol—appears to have fewer negative effects than boldenone, but all manufacturers recommend that the steroids be used only in animals not intended for breeding, and only for horses who have a medical need for more body tissue. If your mare fits these categories, consult your vet and the officials of any sport in which you compete. There is a growing movement to make their use illegal in both equine and human sports. Remember this fact, too: the Colorado State study shows that many mares maintained the negative effects of steroids long after the injections were stopped.

Most conservative horse people would rather choose a mare who already possesses the physical qualities they want, rather then try to create those qualities through potentially dangerous medication. Some mares are naturally more aggressive than others, and some are naturally more heavily muscled and possess heavier necks. Those characteristics can be found in a mare, if you're convinced you need them for a particular sport.

3

The Mental Mare

THE CROWD AT SARATOGA WAS THUNDERSTRUCK BY THE PERFORMANCE
of the five-year-old Lady's Secret, but not in the way that they and
her handlers had expected. Thoroughbred racing's reigning Horse
of the Year was heavily favored in the forty-fifth start of her brilliant
career that August afternoon in 1987. She liked the Saratoga track.
In fact, she had earned her championship honors there largely on
the strength of a victory over older male horses in the prestigious
Whitney Handicap the previous summer. Lady's Secret was
healthy, sound and highly experienced. Her people were hoping to
add to the more than $3 million she had earned in her racing career.

But on August 10, 1987, Lady's Secret neglected to turn left on
the first turn of a modest allowance race and bolted to the outside
fence directly in front of the thousands of fans who had made her
the odds-on favorite. She careened around the racetrack, nearly
bumping against the outside rail on the far side of the track. The
frantic efforts of her jockey, Chris McCarron, and an outrider
brought the distracted Lady's Secret to a stop half a mile after her
bolt.

Nobody knew why it happened. Trainer D. Wayne Lukas told

reporters after Lady's Secret's bizarre display, "If she was human, we'd take her to a psychiatrist." They didn't do that, but they did retire her from racing two months later without her ever making another start. She retired sound, and the only thing anybody seemed to be able to say about her Saratoga performance was "Sometimes mares get that way."

On January 18, 1992, the three-year-old Quarter Horse filly Corona Chick was entered in the La Primera del Año Derby at Los Alamitos in California. The winner's share of the $157,000 purse seemed to be hers for the asking. The morning line had Corona Chick at odds of 1–9, while everybody else in the field was 99–1.

No wonder. She was coming off a two-year-old season more brilliant than any horse had enjoyed in many decades. She had received the most votes in balloting for overall World Champion Quarter Horse, although an odd tabulation rule that discourages two-year-old World Champions gave the title to a four-year-old stallion.

The Derby field seemed at her mercy as she entered the gate. But suddenly, Corona Chick threw herself against the front of her gate stall, bounced off the sides, shook her jockey off and promptly fell under the starting gate. The rest of the horses had to be removed while Corona Chick was extricated. She was scratched at the gate, although her injuries proved not to be serious. The most anybody could say about Corona Chick's escapade was "Sometimes mares get that way."

But sometimes they don't. The Thoroughbred Personal Ensign wound up her thirteen-start career with a victory in the $1 million Breeders' Cup Distaff of 1988. The win made her the first American Thoroughbred in eighty years to complete a full career undefeated. Man o'War and Citation couldn't do it. Secretariat and Native Dancer couldn't do it. The filly Personal Ensign could, because she never had a bad day on the racetrack.

Her accomplishment pales in comparison with that of the Hungarian Thoroughbred Kincsem, who began a fifty-four-race winning streak in 1874. Kincsem traveled throughout Europe by rail and boat, becoming the most accomplished undefeated racehorse in equine history by performing on dozens of different racecourses. Kincsem was a mare and she, too, never had a bad day on the racetrack.

Some mares never "get that way." Or, if they do, it doesn't affect their performance. To be fair, male horses have been known to have spells of irrational behavior as well. But conventional wisdom—as well as the firm belief of many horse people—has it that mares are more likely to be nervous, flighty, moody and subject to alteration in behavior than male horses, particularly geldings.

This may be true, although it's certainly not always so. Just think of Kincsem and her fifty-four straight races. But we have plenty of casual observation to draw upon, as well as limited research. We also have lots of assumptions, some of which appear to be based in something other than reality.

One thing requires no debate: female horses are psychologically different from male horses, just like they are physically different. What we can do is debate whether or not their differences create significant barriers to their performance.

The first step to understanding the psychology of the female horse—of any horse, really—is to understand her role in the natural world. Eons separate the modern horse from the wild horse. Even if your mare came from the Department of the Interior's wild horse adoption program, you have a feral rather than a wild horse, because it is descended from escaped or released domestic animals.

Hippologists believe that the only true wild horse extant is the Przewalski Horse, which lives in Mongolia. It is a member of a different though closely related species of domestic horse. Studies of feral horses in the American West, in Europe and in Asia show that behavior patterns of wild horses of the domestic species are quite similar to those of the Przewalski Horse. Those patterns are the key to understanding the behavior of the horses we live with.

The first and most important fact to remember is that the horse is an herbivore with limited means of self-protection against predators. As a grass-eater, the horse is a prize to meat-eating animals. As the possessor of neither a thick protective coat nor sharp teeth, the horse is vulnerable if caught. This vulnerability has created certain truths about the nature of horses that generations of domestication have been unable to change.

Flight

With its limited ability to fight back against predators, the horse's greatest tool in self-preservation is its speed. The natural response of a horse to a threat is flight, and the horse who sees or hears something frightening wants to run away from it. A well-trained horse probably won't do it, but it will want to. The response of a competition horse to a shout or a loud snap of a whip by a rider may be a result of this compulsion to flee. The rider may be arousing some primitive flight instinct, and the horse runs or trots faster.

All horses share this characteristic to run away from threats, but it's possible that mares feel the urge a little more. The most vulnerable wild horse of all is a foaling mare, followed by a foal, and then a mare with a foal at her side. The mare is less flexible in her escape routes and less able to move quickly. Mares may feel an instinctive urge to flee from a threat sooner than a male horse does.

Observation suggests that many mares do respond more intensely to shouts or cracks of the whip. Most tail-flippers—horses who respond to the whip with a snap of the tail—are female. They don't necessarily slow down to flip their tails, but most trainers and riders would rather their mares use their energy on muscles other than those that move the tail. Some riders and drivers believe that mares are more likely to flip their tails during estrus, but others say they don't see any hormonal pattern to the behavior and believe that it happens in response to the whip or to shouts. Some Standardbred drivers tie fillies' tails to the sulky to stop the flipping.

In most sports, it would be more practical to work out a level of urging that gets the maximum response without prompting tail waving. This may require experimentation and the assistance of a friend at ringside watching as you work and urge your mare.

Fear of Confinement

Closely related to the instinct to flee from danger is the instinctive fear of confinement that seems to be natural to horses. In the wild, confinement means vulnerability, because a confined horse is unable to exercise its best defense against predators.

Most horses do adjust to being led, tied and stabled, since they learn very early that confinement is going to be their lot in life. But they adjust with varying degrees of comfort, probably depending upon how they were handled as very young horses. It's possible that some horses have retained a greater dose of natural equine instincts than others and will always be more uncomfortable and nervous when they feel confined, no matter how carefully they were handled as foals.

There is no way of determining what behavioral problems can be blamed on the equine instinct against confinement, and there is no way to do anything but guess whether there is a difference in the way female and male horses react to it. We do know that pregnant mares will work very hard to foal late at night outside. Careful handlers of broodmares will begin bringing expectant mares inside at night weeks before their due dates, so a clever mare won't sneakily foal in the far reaches of the paddock when nobody is watching. You can't blame her for trying. Instinct tells her that she and her precocious but wobbly foal will be safer if they can get up and run away within an hour or so of the birth.

The instinctive fear of confinement may also play a role in the willingness of mares to work hard at training in sports where concentration is vital. As you will see in later chapters, some trainers in the highly controlled equine sports find that mares are often less willing to give themselves up to the control of their riders and trainers. They find that working to instill a sense of cooperation rather than submission works best with mares.

Safety in Numbers

The vulnerability of the individual wild horse to predators contributed to the development of the natural social structure of the horse. There is safety in numbers for targets of carnivores. At worst, a cougar or coyote might get one member of a herd while the rest escape. At best, the sheer number of herd members might distract the predator from catching even one. In addition, more pairs of eyes and ears make it more likely that a predator will be identified before it strikes.

In domestication, horses have remained highly social. They much prefer the company of other horses to solitude. Lacking members of their own species, they will accept other animals, including humans. In fact, the horse's urge to be sociable is a major part of what makes it amenable to participating in activities with humans.

Again, we can only speculate about whether male or female horses need more companionship. In the wild, males (only stallions, of course) are somewhat more solitary than females. One stallion will handle herds ranging from a handful to dozens of mares and foals. Although they do socialize with mares and foals, they spend much of their nonfeeding and nontraveling time chasing off male competitors or breeding their mares. Stallions unlucky enough to lack mares may be completely solitary, or they may form small, loosely structured herds with other solitary males.

Mares, on the other hand, are rarely solitary. They form distinct, carefully maintained, socially satisfying and mutually protective herds. Observation of feral herds shows that membership remains remarkably constant, with only a few mares leaving to join other herds during the course of a year.

The herd structure is vital for the safety of mares and their foals in the wild. In captivity, contact with other animals may be particularly important for the psychological comfort of fillies and mares, although it is important for male horses, too.

Trainers in all three of the major racing breeds and some of the show disciplines have traditionally used companion animals for any horse who seems to need it, but particularly for nervous fillies. They believe a goat in the stall helps calm nervousness, but the effect may be more basic and specific than that. The goat—or cat or pony—may be satisfying the filly's instinctive urge to be a member of a closely knit herd.

Weaponry

In captivity, horses rarely get involved in real fights with other horses. Owners frown on such activities and make it a point to prevent them. But an understanding of how horses fight in the wild helps us to understand the nature of their occasional aggression toward people and to learn how to protect ourselves from it.

Here's the basic rule: Male horses strike and bite, while female horses kick. That is a vast oversimplification; individual horses can do any or all of these things. But on the whole, the male's favored choice of weapons includes his teeth and his forelegs, while the female's are her heels. Watch out accordingly.

In the wild, a stallion's fighting includes active aggression to take and keep mares from other stallions. He wants to injure or kill his opponent (or to convince the other stallion that he might) to maintain his position.

A mare's fight is usually for protection of herself and her foal. She doesn't particularly want to injure her opponent and is satisfied as long as it leaves her alone. Consequently, her most sensible move is to turn her rump toward a threat and kick out with her rear legs.

This behavior remains in the most thoroughly domesticated horses. It's visible within a few weeks of birth. Colts begin play-striking and nipping—usually with other colts—as very young foals, while fillies play much more gently, just throwing out the occasional rear hoof to assert their positions. Their favorite play activity is running. Fighting interests them far less.

The urge to find safety in numbers is felt by all horses. In the wild, females are more likely than males to develop elaborate social structures made up of members of their own sex.

Mares love companionship, and a wild goose may do if a horse (or another domestic animal) can't be found.

The kick is the weapon of choice for most mares.

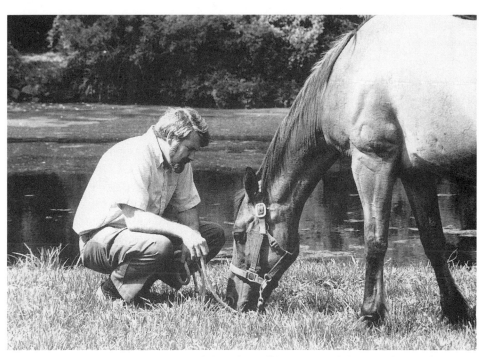

People who care for horses often find themselves talking more to their mares than to their stallions or geldings.

Who's the Boss?

Anybody who pictures an aggressive, possessive wild stallion and assumes that the male is the naturally dominant figure in the horse world assumes wrong. The stallion is dominant to the extent that he gathers and protects his group of mares, but studies of feral horses over the last few decades have turned up a surprise. Most herds have a clear leader—a so-called alpha horse—and some herds have one or more sub-leaders. These administrative positions are almost invariably held by mares.

The job usually goes to an experienced, mature mare, but sometimes a younger mare is bossy enough to usurp the position. The leader, with the advice and consent of sub-leaders, makes virtually all the important decisions of the herd—where to go, when to travel, when to run away from a threat, when to rest. The stallion almost never travels in front of his herd, but rather follows behind or to one side, making sure he doesn't lose any mares on the trip.

This revelation serves as a reminder that we should never assume roles based on sex. A huntsman may feel free to ride a mare. The rest of the horses in the hunt will feel perfectly comfortable following her. Their ancestors did it all the time.

The Senses

There appears to be no substantial difference between the sexes in the structure or functioning of the brain in domestic or wild horses. The female brain may weigh slightly less than the male, since brain size within a species is usually proportional to body size. But this does not affect intelligence or capacity to learn. If a larger brain meant greater intelligence, a Shire would be many times more intelligent than a Shetland pony, and anybody who has met a Shetland knows that this can't possibly be true.

The ability to see and hear appears to be the same in both male and female horses. But some observers are convinced that mares respond to sounds with more interest and more sensitivity than do stallions or geldings. They believe that loud noises are more upsetting to mares and that soothing sounds are more likely to calm them. There's no proof of this, but there is evidence that mares themselves have a wider variety of sounds to call upon for communication. In addition to the various sounds that all horses can make, mares use an extensive and specialized collection of nickers and calls with their foals. Sound communication is used almost immediately after birth and continues as the foal becomes more mobile. Sound is important to the foal's safety and security since he cannot yet see, and sound helps him locate his dam.

Many professional riders speak more to mares than they do to geldings or stallions, even though they sometimes don't know they are doing it. Some jockeys carry on a starting-gate-to-wire conversation with fillies, particularly young ones, in an effort to calm and focus them. Grooms, too, often find themselves talking more to their female charges.

Trainers, particularly those who handle racing Standardbreds, often resort to ear muffs or ear plugs to muffle the loud or sudden sounds that upset some mares. The muffling devices are also used on stallions and geldings, but they do seem to be more common on mares. The object is not to block out all sounds, but rather to reduce the impact of the noises—such as a roaring crowd or the crack of another driver's whip—that frighten particularly sensitive mares. A bunched-up piece of foam rubber placed carefully in the ear can do the trick. Ready-made ear muffs are also available.

Estrus

All mares, wild or domestic, share a characteristic that always and forever sets them apart from stallions and geldings. From the age of about eighteen months until the day she dies, almost every mare who hasn't lost her ovaries through surgery, disease or drug damage goes through spells described variously as "heat," "season," "horsing" or, in the words of some racetrackers, "filly trouble." The proper name is estrus, and the condition is accepted with varying degrees of dread and tolerance by people who own mares.

The late Hall-of-Fame driver Ralph Baldwin used a carefully made ear hood on the trotter Kimberly Dutchess. (Photo credit: USTA)

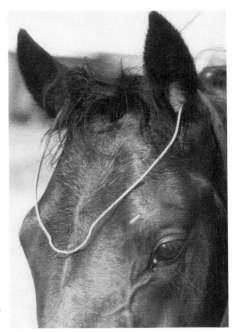

Even a simple set of foam plugs can help muffle startling noises. (Photo credit: USTA)

Estrus, the period of a mare's reproductive cycle in which she can be bred and conceive, is a physiological process, but its psychological effects are of great concern to people who use mares for sport and leisure. The condition is blamed for nearly every behavioral quirk that any mare has ever displayed, even though mares are *not* in season for a much greater percentage of their lives than they *are* in season.

Estrus makes a convenient scapegoat. It's easier to accept than errors in early training, and easier to understand than innate character flaws. Moreover, estrus often really is responsible for a mare acting up. Often, but not always, and that's what we have to remember.

The true role of estrus in mare behavior becomes even more difficult to determine, especially since mares show much greater variation than females of other species in both their cycles and the effects of those cycles on their physical and mental condition. The reproductive health of mares is a topic of intensive and ongoing research in equine veterinary medicine. Still, what we do know about estrus tells us that raging hormones do not rule the life of the female horse.

When Does It Occur?

The horse, both male and female, is highly light-sensitive in terms of its reproductive abilities. Breeding, with few exceptions, occurs only when days are longer than nights. In the Northern Hemisphere, that means that the natural breeding season runs from late March through late September. Nature likes to be even more specific. Left to their own devices, stallions are most likely to breed mares during the late spring and early summer, suggesting that their bodies give them an internal signal to breed about eleven months before food supplies are likely to be most plentiful.

The stallion remains fertile year round, but stallions tend to have little interest in breeding during the winter months. Mares go well beyond that.

Not only do normal mares have no interest in breeding during cold weather, they couldn't become pregnant if they did. Although there are exceptions, the great majority of mares will not come into heat between late September and late March. This is called the anestrous period. Many mares won't even come into heat throughout the entire six months of long days, but will limit themselves to about three months in the middle of that period.

That means, if your mare is average, you may have to worry about her coming into season only about one-quarter of the year. Unfortunately for owners of performance mares, that three-month period comes in late spring and early summer, which often coincides with the most important shows and race meets of the year.

The news isn't much better for owners of pleasure mares, since prime estrus time is also prime riding time. In the midwestern United States the most likely time for estrus is May, June and July. But there is tremendous variation among individual mares, even members of the same breed. Some come into season like clockwork every three weeks for six months, while others never seem to be interested in breeding at all. But the owner of the average mare will be able to blame estrus for any quirks in her behavior for only three or four months a year.

How Long Does It Last?

Even during those three or four months (or five or six, if your mare isn't average), she is not constantly under the influence of her reproductive desires. The normal equine reproductive cycle lasts about twenty-one days, although it can be shorter or longer.

For the typical mare, those three weeks work out like this: fifteen days of diestrus, in which she is unwilling to be bred and cannot conceive, followed by five days of estrus, in which she should be willing to be bred, and one end-of-the-cycle day, in which either a sperm fertilizes an egg and makes the mare pregnant or does not and she goes back into diestrus. Her willingness to be bred that day varies from mare to mare and from cycle to cycle.

So the average mare is in heat only five or six days every three weeks during three to six months of the year, usually closer to three months. That means estrus is likely to affect a mare's behavior only twenty-five to fifty total days a year. In a few cases, usually at the beginning or end of the breeding season, a mare might be in heat for a month, or she might be in diestrus for only a day. But most mares will follow something resembling the three-week cycle.

Diestrus is not the same as anestrus. During the fall and winter, a mare who is approached by a stallion usually shows no interest. During breeding season, providing she isn't in heat, she may be more active in her disapproval, probably kicking and squealing at a stallion's approach. Otherwise, a diestrous mare behaves pretty much the same as she does when she is anestrous. But an estrous mare is something else altogether.

Estrus and Behavior

What does estrus do to behavior? There is no easy answer to this question because every mare is different. Some show no outward signs whatsoever, even to an interested stallion. Internal palpation by a veterinarian is the only way to determine estrus in undemonstrative mares.

Others show the effects of estrus only when approached by a stallion. These mares will raise their tails, urinate, "wink" their vulvas, squat or make other movements to respond to the stallion. When there is no stallion around, some estrous mares will offer the same display to a gelding or even to another mare.

Some mares show distinct behavioral changes regardless of the presence or absence of a stallion. Some of these changes may be unpleasant and others may actually be enjoyable. None of the changes, though, is likely to make the estrous mare a better performer.

Some mares become grouchy when they're in heat. They don't like to be in their stalls, they don't like to be bridled, they don't like to work. Their bodies are telling them to find themselves a stallion, and any other activity seems like a waste of time.

Other mares become affectionate. Lacking a stallion, they will flirt with geldings, cows or people. They will nuzzle, rub, nibble

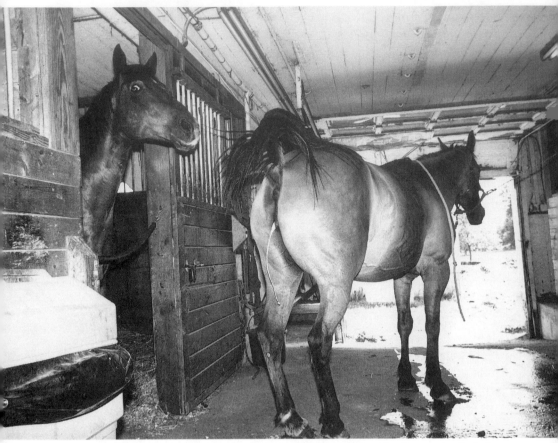

Brandy may be twenty-six years old and a gelding, but Annie's estrus antics (including squatting, winking and urinating) are aimed directly at him.

and demand to be scratched. This kind of estrous mare can be a joy, provided you don't expect her to concentrate on her work. She won't concentrate, she won't learn and she will forget what she has already learned. She will enjoy being petted, though.

Controlling Estrus

What can you do to control estrus? First, what you can't do. You can't punish a mare for something she is unable to control. No, you don't have to let her bolt, or stop in the middle of the road because she spots a potential stallion across a field, or refuse to come into her stall during a lightning storm. Yes, you can stop her from nipping or insist she do at least some work. But you should never be rough with her because of heat-induced grouchiness or be annoyed into giving her more than just a quick firm reprimand for misbehavior.

You can try to learn her cycle—if she's thoughtful enough to be regular—and plan your schedule around it. You can also learn what constitutes typical estrous behavior for her. If she's difficult only in the presence of stallions, try to use her only with geldings or other mares. If estrus makes her nervous in crowds, try to avoid them. Some mares kick only when in heat.

If she behaves well but doesn't seem to be able to learn anything, schedule the introduction of new skills for a later training session. Although mares differ in their heat behavior, each individual tends to follow her own patterns. Careful observation during a few estrous cycles will give you an idea of what to expect.

But what can you do if you can't alter her schedule? What if the most important show of the year falls right in the middle of the breeding season? What if your mare forgets everything when she's in heat? Can you stop estrus?

Yes, but don't consider it without consulting an equine vet, preferably one who handles broodmares and reproduction. There are several drugs on the market that suppress estrus. Most were developed to regulate the cycles of mares who had trouble cycling or ovulating—mares whose owners wanted to encourage rather than suppress estrus. The primary drug used to stop a mare from coming into season is based on progesterone, a hormone produced by the ovaries of every normal mare. It is usually effective and safe, although some mares can suffer allergic or injection reactions to the administration of the drug. These are usually not serious.

When the medication is stopped, a strong estrus is supposed to occur. Owners eager to get a mare in foal hurry her off to the stallion at this point. Owners of performance mares have to just wait the heat out. Presumably, the estrus won't be allowed to appear until after the big race or the important show. Trainers of performance mares—particularly those who compete in jumping and dressage—have used these drugs with great success, some for months at a time. There are questions, though, about how long these drugs can reasonably be used before allowing estrus to occur, and they should never be used without veterinary supervision.

Anabolic steroids may also suppress estrus in many mares, but they might cause a mare to behave far worse than she might if she came into heat. What's more, her future breeding potential might be compromised. That is a high price to pay for the avoidance of a few days of heat.

There is constant and well-financed research into equine reproduction underway at veterinary centers throughout the United States, and we are bound to learn more about estrus control in the future. A large-animal vet with an interest in broodmare care will be able to advise you about new drugs as they reach the market, should you feel you can't alter your plans to suit your mare's reproductive cycle.

Here is one more anti-estrus trick. Since the breeding season is light induced, breeders who want early foals have known for years that they can encourage early cycling by placing mares under artificial light starting in early winter. When the hours of daylight and artificial light total about sixteen hours a day, a mare can be induced to begin coming in season in late January.

The opposite probably works, too. If you want to put off cycling as long as possible, be careful about how many hours you keep the lights on in the barn and how strong a light bulb you use. This does not mean you can delay cycling indefinitely by keeping your mare in a dark stable. Her mental and physical health demand light, preferably sunlight. You just don't have to supplement what nature provides.

The Human Factor in Mare Behavior

Sometimes mares "act that way" not because of genetic preprogramming, or hormones, or anything else inside them. Sometimes the fault lies with the people who own and handle them. People, being intelligent creatures who learn from experience, know that female horses are different from male horses and handle them accordingly. When this different kind of handling begins at birth, the female horse will become different, whether nature intended her to or not. If it continues during early training and is maintained during adult use, the difference may become permanent.

How We Treat the Mare

Most professional and serious amateur breeders will claim that fillies are not treated differently from birth, and some of them are telling the truth. Others, no matter how convinced they are that they handle their male and female foals identically, do show subtle differences in their treatment of fillies and colts. Sometimes the differences don't occur until some time after weaning, when the colts and fillies are separated forever. Others think it's important to handle foals according to sex within a day of birth.

A Thoroughbred farm in Florida foals a hundred mares each spring, and postpartum mares are turned out in paddocks according to the sex of their foals. The farm has a good reason for this. Within a week or two, colts start to play rougher than fillies. While colts do concentrate on same-sex playmates for their mock fights, the broodmare manager thinks colts sometimes make mistakes and can frighten or endanger the fillies.

Late in the summer, weaning begins with the colts. The manager likes to get colts away from their dams before the age of five months, because the occasional colt shows sexual behavior very young and can be badly kicked if he tries to mount his dam. The fillies may be weaned up to several weeks later.

Does the age of weaning affect the ultimate personality or behavior of the colts and fillies? It's hard to say. This particular farm has had success with both. The best-known graduates of the farm have been colts, but that is hardly an unusual situation on a Thoroughbred breeding farm. But certainly the amount of handling a foal receives during its impressionable early months has an effect on its relationship to humans and probably on its trainability.

The manager of a Standardbred farm in upstate New York believes that his fillies and colts are treated the same from birth—each is haltered the morning after foaling and is taught to lead within days—but even he acknowledges that colts tend to get a little more attention because of their rambunctiousness. Again, there is no way to know if this extra early attention makes the colts more inclined to accept control and to tolerate the rigors of competition when they become adult horses.

Research and experience tells us that all horses adjust better to their ultimate lives as adult equine athletes if they get used to human presence and human handling from the first few days of their lives, provided the handling is gentle and nonthreatening. It's important for owners of fillies to not make the mistake of thinking their foals don't need attention because they are quieter and better behaved than colts.

It is true that it's more natural to leave a foal alone with its mother, not touching it or handling it until weaning time. But the modern foal is not destined for a natural life. A filly needs at least as much human contact as a colt if she is to be expected to perform as comfortably as he does as the partner of a human being.

Ask for Less, Get Less

How much work a horse in training needs, and how physically and mentally demanding that work should be, cannot be answered easily. There is no agreement about the ideal age for training to

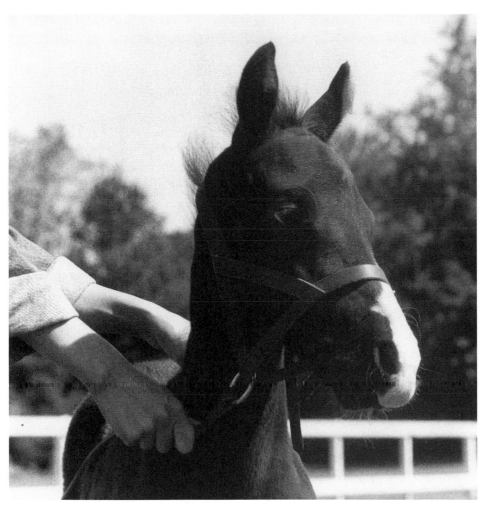

Fillies as well as colts must be haltered, handled and accustomed to humans early, if they're going to react to later training in a similar manner.

begin, about how heavy a weight a young horse can carry and about how much mileage you can put on young legs.

Research provides us with conflicting evidence. For example, two major studies on racetrack breakdowns were completed during the late 1980s at two different racetracks. The first showed that young horses—two- and three-year-olds—were more likely to suffer serious racing injuries. The second showed that horses four and older were more likely to suffer fatal or career-ending injuries. It's hard to draw conclusions about age and heavy use from results like that.

People who start jumpers also debate the ideal age to begin jumping, and how much jumping a young horse can do. Some think that horses who start late last longer. European trainers tend to think horses should not be put into serious training until at least the age of four or five, resulting in international careers that don't begin until the age of nine or ten. Of course, there's no universal agreement in Europe. The German mare Classic Touch became an Olympic Gold medalist at the age of eight. The great British horse Milton, who started late, seemed well past his peak for the 1992 Olympics at the age of fourteen. Supporters of an early start point to the great Thoroughbred Grand Prix jumpers, horses like Idle Dice, Jet Run and For The Moment, who lasted well into their late teens on the show circuit, even though they were broken as yearlings and used steadily in one sport or another from then on.

Training programs for adult horses also come under scrutiny. At what point do ring work and galloping or lungeing become counterproductive? When does the horse no longer learn and improve but rather become sour? Those questions—and the questions about training young animals—have to be answered by each trainer according to his or her knowledge and experience of training in general and the nature of his own horse in particular.

But there seems little question about this: If you have two horses of similar age and health in training for a particular sport, and you spend less time working with one because she is a "delicate" filly, you will probably get a mare who's less competent and less skilled than her male training mate.

This does not mean you should put your 200-pound body on your 750-pound two-year-old filly just because your 1,000-pound colt can carry you. It does mean that you shouldn't assume that she can't concentrate for an hour of training while the colt can. It does mean that she can go for as long a walk-trot hack as he can, provided the size of the rider is suitable for her frame and musculature.

In fact, in most breeds, fillies appear to mature more quickly than colts. They cut back on play behavior sooner than colts. Most mares reach puberty, attain their adult size and get their adult mouths anywhere from two months to a year sooner than male horses of the same breed. Fillies may actually be physically and mentally ready for training earlier than colts and geldings.

As for adult horses, there is no evidence that mares are mentally less capable of concentrating than geldings, except for the handful of days during the year that they are in heat. There is plenty of evidence that mares should be able to concentrate on their work better than stallions, who are fertile and at least marginally interested in breeding year round.

There is a possibility that unaltered horses—male and female—are more observant of the world around them because they are closer to the "natural" horse that has to both protect itself against predators and look for mates. This characteristic may be interpreted as an inability to concentrate, but it may in fact mean that the unneutered horse is just more easily distracted. The distinction is important, because distraction is something that horse, trainer and rider can learn to deal with, while a true inability to concentrate is not.

Here's the rule: If you expect less of a horse in training, you will get less. In some cases, a mare who performs a little less competently than a male horse from the same background is simply a victim of a self-fulfilling prophecy.

Rewarding Bad Behavior

You may say you would never reward bad behavior. But how about when your mare tenses up in fear at a yappy dog or loud noise or strange person? Don't you pat her neck, murmur sweet nothings to her and gently praise her for being a good girl and just wheeling rather than bolting? Of course you do! Since mares tend to be nervous, they need the love and reassurance, don't they? Wrong.

What you do when you praise and pat a horse who's gotten herself into a nervous frenzy over the sight of your neighbor is to reinforce her behavior. She has learned that she's petted if she acts like a nervous wreck.

People who love horses are inclined to do this for any frightened horse, male or female. But the pervasive feeling that mares are indeed nervous makes them a more common target of misplaced petting and praise. In addition, mares may be a little more likely to be petted and cuddled anyway, just because they're female (if you don't believe it, watch good professional grooms with their charges—they'll often be all over their mares and gentle but matter-of-fact with their geldings).

A nervous mare—or nervous horse of any kind—should never be praised for her nervousness. She can be reassured by being spoken to gently by her rider. She can be calmed with a hand on the withers. She can be praised if she handles her nervousness by quietly examining the terrifying piece of paper that blew in front of her. But she should not be told that she has done what her rider wants when she has stopped short or bucked or bolted in fear.

Many riders unwittingly reinforce the reputations that mares have for nervousness by expecting and even rewarding nervousness when it occurs. Hormones and natural history have contributed enough potential problems to mare behavior without adding human-caused problems to the mix.

4

The Racing Mare

PEOPLE WHO WORK AT RACETRACKS DON'T OFTEN CRY OVER HORSES; they probably wouldn't last long if they were the kind of people who did. They couldn't take the losing that comes so much more regularly than the winning. Nor could they take watching horses come and go as frequently and as quickly as they do. At a place where speed seems so often to go hand in hand with fragility, and where a long career might be two seasons and twenty-five races, people fight sentiment. But sometimes they fail.

For trainer D. Wayne Lukas, the tears came on a December morning in 1982. Lukas was highly experienced, highly successful and tough. He was known as a no-nonsense trainer who expected a lot from his horses, his employees and himself. No horse gave him more than Landaluce, a two-year-old filly whose brief career could have been defined by the word "perfection." Five starts and five easy wins had Lukas dreaming of Horse of the Year honors. Victories in two planned races—one against colts—could have clinched the title for the dark bay filly.

Landaluce ran a fever early in the month, got better, then worse. Antibiotics didn't seem to help. The title no longer mattered; the fight now was to save her life from the infection that raged through her body. Landaluce and Lukas lost that fight, too. The dark bay filly died during the early morning hours of December 12, her head in her trainer's lap.

Later that morning, while announcing her death to reporters, Lukas cried over the fallen filly. In the years since then, he has trained numerous champions—most of them fillies and mares—but he has never quite forgotten Landaluce. He has lost other good horses, but none has had the impact that she did.

The racetrack is a tough place, and horses sometimes don't survive the challenges. Thoroughbreds are bred to run up to and beyond the limits of their bodies, and the best of them do it with breathtaking determination. Both males and females are vulnerable, and no significant study has shown fillies or mares more likely to suffer breakdown or life-threatening illness.

In fact, leading California trainer Gary Jones believes the opposite may be true. Jones, trainer of such outstanding mares as Kostroma, Beautiful Glass, Comedy Act, and Heart of Joy, says, "I think male horses have a slightly higher percentage of breakdowns. They carry more flesh, and that's what increases the concussion. Concussion, along with fatigue, causes breakdown." Jones does not believe that the slightly heavier bone structure makes up for the weight disadvantage that males have in terms of breakdowns.

Still, it seems that the fillies and mares bring the tears. I had never seen Landaluce and, at the time, had never met the people connected with her. But while reporting her death on a national sports network telecast the night of December 12, 1982, I started to cry and couldn't finish the story. Eighteen months later, Kentucky Derby and Belmont Stakes winner Swale, a wonderful colt whom I had seen race half a dozen times and whose people I knew and admired, died unexpectedly. I was heartbroken, but I got through the story of his death with no problem. Who can explain it?

The Special Bond with Racing Fillies

Many people—handlers, friends and strangers—have a special affection for good fillies and mares, a fondness that often exceeds what they feel for equally good male horses. The fillies don't become media stars any more often than male horses do, but they do become the objects of great emotional attachment. Perhaps it's the contrast—the idea that something female could perform so well. Perhaps it's the idea that you somehow tempt fate when you campaign a good filly. Fear brings extra joy to success. Statistics may claim otherwise, but it does seem that the most devastating losses have been of fillies and mares. They have certainly brought the most tears.

Nearly twenty-five years after her death in 1963, the trainer of the lovely Lamb Chop would describe the horrors of her breakdown and subsequent death on a California track and shake his head. He remembered the tears of everybody who worked in his barn and thousands of people at the racetrack. The young champion was like a Dresden figurine, and it was the loss of her beauty as well as her spirit and talent that people mourned.

In 1990 two-time champion Go For Wand, a model of consistency and soundness in her two-year racing career, broke down on the lead in a Breeders' Cup race at Belmont Park. When she was destroyed a few minutes later, many of the more than 50,000 people at the track and the 3.4 million people in the television audience were crying over her loss. Even the trainer of the mare who inherited the win in the million-dollar race shed tears in the winner's circle.

But no loss compares to that of Ruffian, the shooting star of a filly whose career was probably the most extraordinary of any horse of modern times. Ten starts, ten easy wins, ten times breaking or tying either a track or stakes record. No horse ever put a head in front of Ruffian in a race—not until a couple of strides after she shattered the bones in her ankle in the infamous 1975 match race with the colt Foolish Pleasure.

She carried extraordinary public acclaim into that race, including the admiration and affection of a lot of people who previously knew

Ruffian was fast, big and powerful, but her death in 1975 following a match race against a colt, Foolish Pleasure, helped solidify the notion that female horses are not quite competitive with males. (Photo credit: NYRA)

nothing about horses or racing. She was so compelling mostly because of her unique talent. But a significant part of her glory was her sex. When she died following surgery the next morning, tears were shed. Tears still come to many people on the day of two of Belmont Park's most important events, the Belmont Stakes and the Ruffian Handicap, when they realize that fresh flowers in the black filly's red and white racing colors have been placed on her infield grave.

Ruffian's death had a profound impact on people and on the sport. For one thing, there has not been a match race between top level horses since. Whenever somebody brings up the possibility, the name of Ruffian is invoked and the would-be participants find a regularly scheduled race to enter.

But the tragic match race did something else. It revived the centuries-old argument over whether racing fillies and mares are as fast as male horses. If they were as fast, are they equally good as race horses? And even if they are as good, should they compete against males? The debate intensified after 1975, but the answers are no more clear than they were before then. Statistics don't necessarily lie, but they don't always tell the entire truth.

Female Horses and Speed

Are female horses as fast as males? Nobody knows. It's as simple as that. In Thoroughbred racing, a race time is not always an accurate indicator of quality. A field of claiming horses might run six furlongs in 1 minute 10 seconds, while a field of stakes horses might run the same distance the next day in 1 minute 11 seconds. If you match the two winners ten times, the stakes winner will probably beat the claiming horse ten times. The time of the race reflects the strategy of the race and the track surface at least as much as it does the innate speed of the competitors.

Still, unless every horse is matched head to head against every other horse, time is the best thing we have with which to judge speed. Time certainly gave Ruffian's handlers reason to think she could handle Foolish Pleasure. The filly had won the 12-furlong

Coaching Club American Oaks in a time ⅖ second faster than Avatar had run the Belmont Stakes on the same track a couple of weeks before, a race in which Foolish Pleasure was second. She had won the 9-furlong Mother Goose Stakes in a time ⅗ second faster than Foolish Pleasure had won the Flamingo Stakes, at the same distance. The summer before, Ruffian had run the 6-furlong Sorority Stakes at Monmouth Park a full 1⅖ seconds faster than Foolish Pleasure ran the 6-furlong Sapling at the same track. Ruffian was almost certainly faster than Foolish Pleasure, but she died trying to beat the colt.

It's not uncommon for fillies and mares to run their same-sex races in faster times than equivalent open races, usually won by male horses. It happens at all distances and at all tracks, although not all the time.

Fillies and mares fare well in open competitions based on sheer speed. They have an excellent record, for example, in Belmont Park's 6-furlong Fall Highweight Handicap, which usually plays a major role in determining which horse is named champion sprinter. Winners Chou Croute, Gold Beauty, Honorable Miss, Ta Wee (who won once carrying 130 pounds, once with 140), could run as fast as anybody.

Female horses hold a number of world, American and Canadian records, mostly at very short and very long distances. For some unexplained reason, their performances are particularly good in turf racing. Most championship honors are divided according to sex: There is a champion two-year-old colt and a champion two-year-old filly, for example. But there is just one sprint champion, and that title goes to a mare about a third of the time. There are mares fast enough to win more often than that, but a mare with easy pickings in same-sex races may never be given a chance to win the open races she needs to earn a championship.

On balance, fillies and mares are probably pretty close to male horses in terms of sheer speed, particularly at the shorter distances. But they don't win the big open races nearly as often as males do, and that brings up the question that really matters to owners and admirers of mares.

Mares vs. Colts in Racing

Are mares as good at racing as colts? Maybe not. The weight of statistics don't tell the whole story. But if mares are less successful in direct comparison to males, the reasons are far more complex than simple physical inferiority. Moreover, mares are actually more successful in open competition than they might appear at first glance. If they're not quite as good, they are not much worse.

It's true that only three fillies have won the Kentucky Derby in nearly 120 runnings of the race. Not so good? Actually, figured in terms of winners or placed horses from starters, fillies have done far better than colts and geldings. A third of the fillies who have been entered in the Derby have brought home a paycheck. You can hardly say that of the colts.

Churchill Downs fans know better than to ignore fillies at the betting windows. A two-filly entry was favored in 1984, and Winning Colors, the Derby winner of 1988, was a very close second choice to a colt. She had earned her near-favorite status honestly, having devastated a field of good colts the previous month in the Santa Anita Derby. It took a son of Ruffian's only sister to take the favorite's role from her. She won; he was unplaced. Winning Colors belonged in the Kentucky Derby and proved it.

Winning Colors was an exceptional filly, but she wasn't much— if any—better than some other fillies she faced during her racing career. Six months after her Kentucky Derby victory, she was beaten in the Breeders' Cup by Personal Ensign, a filly who came back from a fractured leg to complete the first full unbeaten career of any American racehorse in more than eighty years. Personal Ensign, running with five screws in her left leg, had won Saratoga's Whitney Handicap against older male horses three months before capping her perfect thirteen-for-thirteen career in the Breeders' Cup.

Lady's Secret, Horse of the Year in 1986 and 1992 Hall of Fame inductee, also beat male horses in the Whitney, although most of her world-record earnings were won in races for fillies and mares. Her brilliant forty-five-race career ended on a sour note with an

Winning Colors' victory in the 1988 Santa Anita Derby earned her the role as second choice in the Kentucky Derby a month later. Her subsequent win shouldn't have come as a surprise to anyone. (Photo credit: Santa Anita Park, Four Footed Fotos)

Personal Ensign, who was retired in 1988, is the only American horse, male or female, since 1908 to complete a full racing career undefeated. (Photo credit: NYRA)

Lady's Secret dominated her own division, but she needed a victory over male horses in New York to earn Horse of the Year honors in 1986. (Photo credit: NYRA)

Jockey Chris McCarron finds that potentially tense mares, such as the brilliant sprinter Heart of Joy, respond to talking and deliberate distractions.

inexplicable bolt in a minor race at Saratoga in 1987, but in the forty-four races before that, she proved that she was as tough, fast and talented as any male horse in training.

Winning Colors, Personal Ensign and Lady's Secret were exceptions, not just in their talent but in their opportunities. Part of the reason fillies and mares don't fare as well as male horses lies in the fact that they often don't get the same chances. Here's why.

Breeding

The quality of the pedigree foreshadows racing talent much more accurately than it does any other equine sporting ability. Speed is the most consistently transmitted talent of all. There are exceptions, but far more good racehorses are well bred than they are poorly bred. This fact lessens the racing opportunities of well-bred fillies.

Many fewer stallions than mares are required by breeders. Even in Thoroughbred racing, where artificial insemination and embryo transfer are not permitted, the average stallion can handle a book of fifty mares per year. Most cover fewer mares, but theoretically you need only one stallion for every fifty mares. Racing record of the parent is at least equal to pedigree in predicting the racing quality of offspring. With comparatively so few stallions needed, a legitimate stud prospect must have both a good pedigree and a good racing record to compete in the stallion marketplace.

Not so with mares. You need fifty times the number of mares, and you can't be quite so particular. Breeders love to have mares with both good pedigrees and good racing records, but one or the other will do. If they can manage only one in their mares, they'll usually take the pedigree. Conventional wisdom has it that pedigree is more important in making a broodmare than racing record. Statistics actually tend to show otherwise, but conventional wisdom dies hard.

A filly with a top pedigree is considered an excellent broodmare prospect, and somebody who owns one is reluctant to do anything to jeopardize her breeding potential. They dread racetrack accidents. Many fillies bred to run and win receive little chance to do either, particularly if they are of a physical type and running style that gets good at the age of four or five. Breeders usually want to start breeding by then.

Throughout the twentieth century, many of the mares who have won a lot of races over several seasons—or who have been "risked" in open competition—have been mares with pedigrees that were not entirely fashionable. A collapse in the bloodstock market in the late 1980s did lead to the realization on the part of owners that they could earn more money by keeping a well-bred good mare in training for an extra year than they could from selling a foal out of her. That kept some fine mares racing longer than they might have in the 1970's. On the whole, though, the best-bred fillies are not campaigned nearly as hard as the best-bred colts, and that undoubtedly accounts for the fact that fillies and mares do not appear to race quite as well as male horses.

Sex Problems

Uncastrated male horses are difficult to handle, especially as they get older, but they rarely have physical problems related to their sex. The occasional ridgling, whose undescended testicles cause discomfort, needs an operation to relieve his pain, but most male horses are not directly affected by their gender.

That is not true with many female racehorses. Trainer Gary Jones says, "You see a lot of mares with ovary problems—even those who've never been on steroids. They get cysts, they don't ovulate right. When they do, sometimes they get stiff and sore behind. They try to compensate, and they're uncomfortable. Several times a year I'll have to palpate a mare who's swishing her tail or who's stiff, to see if there's a problem with her ovaries."

Jones is not a great believer in medication to control estrus, but he will use it in problem mares who are suffering discomfort. "You hate to have to do anything," he says, "but these mares only have so many years they can race. You have to do something for them, and the drugs really seem to relieve them."

Gary Jones worries more about the physical effects of cycling than the effect of estrus on a mare's attitude. "I had one mare who always ran her best when she came in season. She'd wring her tail, but she'd run faster."

Mares often require more observation and care because of medical problems due to their sex. Not every trainer is as watchful as Jones is.

Handling

Trainers who succeed with fillies and mares in both same-sex and open competition tend to handle their female charges differently from their colts and geldings. But it's a fine line between a different style of handling that maximizes performance and one that develops a less fit and skilled athlete.

Gary Jones believes that the first step is to look at the horse as an athlete. "I've had some fillies that are nervous and lighter-bodied than the colts, and they don't need as much work to stay fit. But the best fillies I've had have been tough. They like to train and they can take it. They're all individuals, and you train them according to what they need, whichever sex they are." He says he doesn't make assumptions about what his horses need until he discovers their individual physical requirements.

But Jones—and most successful handlers of racing females—believes that the mind of the mare is what requires a different approach. "You have to spend more time with them than you do colts, especially the good mares," he says. "They tend to want to do everything at their own pace, and they don't like to be pushed around. Once you realize this preference and then come to understand their individual personalities, fillies become easy to train."

It's not easy to get to know the personality of a filly, Jones believes. "They're much more individualistic than males," he says. "There may be only three or four personality categories that you can fit colts into, but there might be twenty types of mares."

Gary Jones succeeds with mares in part because he enjoys this exploration of personality. To him, the challenge is a pleasure, not a problem. "There's nothing better than a great mare," he says.

Other trainers feel differently, becoming frustrated by estrus, by personality quirks, by stubbornness in the face of trainer pressure. These trainers tend not to succeed with mares and probably urge their owners to send them off to the breeding shed.

Money

Most racetracks schedule a more-or-less equal number of races open to both sexes and those exclusively for female horses. There are a very few males-only races, primarily for two-year-olds, but these are rapidly disappearing. The females-only races run the gamut from the cheapest of claiming events to rich stakes.

The stakes races are not quite as rich as the open ones. Gary Jones, with his barn full of good mares, says, "There's too much discrimination as far as I'm concerned. We put too much into the purses for males and not enough for females." He has a point. Bettors pay the bills, and they bet just as happily on races for fillies and mares as on the others. The results are every bit as consistent, with the favorites in filly races winning just about as often as the favorites in open races.

To be fair, fillies and mares are not excluded from the open races, so the richer purses are available to them, too. But few enter, and the money available in female-only races is part of the reason. Filly and mare races prohibit, by definition, half the horses at the racetrack. The competition is inevitably easier, and although the purses may not be quite as good, they are still plentiful. The owner of a good mare cannot be blamed for going after three-quarters as much purse money in a field half as hard. That's good arithmetic.

Lady's Secret won more than $3 million racing mostly in female-only competition. The Breeders' Cup Distaff is currently the only million-dollar race exclusively for fillies and mares, but there are plenty that offer several hundred thousand dollars in purses. A mare can get very rich never venturing out of her own division. Add to this the fact that top racehorses only start a dozen or so times a year, and it's entirely understandable that owners and trainers usually keep their charges in same-sex races.

The Jockey's Perspective

Jockeys spend less time with individual horses than do grooms, trainers or even hotwalkers. They hop aboard ten minutes before the race, run for a minute or two, then spend five minutes coming back. That works out to less than twenty minutes every three or four weeks.

But those twenty minutes are vital to the ultimate success of the horse. Most jockeys will tell you that they don't handle fillies and mares any differently than they do male horses, but the fact is that some jockeys do seem to get more out of them than other riders do.

Jockey Chris McCarron succeeds with virtually any kind of horse. He rode the legendary gelding John Henry, who reached his peak at nine, and the brilliant colt Alysheba, who won millions at three and four. But many of his best mounts have been mares, including champions Lady's Secret, Glorious Song, Life's Magic, Estrapade and Bayakoa. He doesn't necessarily do any better with fillies than colts, but he does something very right with them. Trainers love to use him on their good fillies and mares.

McCarron is concerned about the mentality of the horses he rides. "I don't just get on and ride," he says. "I try to get into their heads a little, and that seems particularly beneficial with fillies. You have to spend more time finding out what makes them go."

McCarron finds that almost all horses respond to talking. "I do a lot of talking to all my horses," he says. "Sometimes the pony people look at me a little funny, but I really feel I get along better with the horses when I do. As soon as I get on them, I start talking to them. I think it makes them more cooperative."

McCarron does find that many fillies are more nervous than colts, although he doesn't think the percentage of nervous animals is much higher with females than males. He does think the tense ones some- times need special treatment. "I do try to be more patient with a nervous horse than a horse who may be stubborn or studdish. If a filly is mean rather than nervous, I will do something to show her who's boss, maybe growl at her or tap her on the shoulder with my stick to get her attention. With a truly nervous one, I might try to get her away from the other horses for a few minutes. She'll get to looking around at the sights and it takes her mind off her nervousness."

This technique helped McCarron make the Gary Jones–trained Heart of Joy into a multiple winner against male sprinters at Santa Anita. She was nervous, but McCarron would ride her uphill to the starting gate of the sprint course where she could see the crowd but not the other horses.

McCarron thinks riders in all disciplines should pay attention to the mentality of mares they ride. "Spend the time to find out what they like and don't like," he advises. "If you can keep her happy, she'll perform well for you."

The Other Racing Sports

Thoroughbred racing gets the majority of the media attention, but other racing sports draw millions of fans, offer many millions of dollars in prize money and provide sometimes greater and sometimes lesser opportunities for mares to prove their talent. In the biggest of the non-Thoroughbred sports, the role of the mare has long been a source of speculation and mystery.

Harness Racing

Harness racing today is like Thoroughbred racing in terms of the role of mares in open competition. Fillies and mares usually race against each other. The purses are just fine, and the competition is halved in filly and mare events. A well-bred Standardbred mare, like the Thoroughbred, does not need a race record to be a good broodmare prospect.

Since time in Standardbred racing is much more indicative of racing ability than it is in Thoroughbred racing, a broodmare should have a respectable time record to enhance the value of her offspring. But she can earn that in a controlled time trial or in a female-only race. Only the lure of very large purses and the occasional twinge of sporting instinct sends fillies and mares into open races. Even then, it almost invariably occurs in just one of harness racing's two subdivisions.

Pacing females almost never compete against males because they are not as fast as male horses of their own level. A stakes-quality pacing mare could beat an allowance or claiming-level colt or gelding, but she almost certainly could not beat a male horse who normally competes at a similar stakes level. At small tracks with few good races, a mare may be dropped down a level or so and race against males so she can make enough starts to earn her way.

But trotting females can and do compete against males. They appear in open races less often as the years go by, since there is a constantly increasing number of lucrative races restricted to females. But when a good filly trotter ventures beyond her division, she's not out of place and few racing fans are surprised. After all, she has a lot of history behind her.

Trotting

Farmers and sportsmen began racing their harness horses on country roads in both Europe and North America as soon as the roads became good enough for their animals to be able to reach racing speed. Not surprisingly, longer distances and straighter, newer roads made the activity more popular in America, and it was in the Middle Atlantic States that organized harness racing began its recorded history in the 1820s. Actually, many of the races were conducted under saddle, but the harness horse's gait was maintained. These were trotting races, contested by horses who could trot nearly as fast as they could run.

From the beginning, male and female horses were used without prejudice about their sex. We read the stories in the old sporting journals and see names like Jersey Kate, Betsey Baker, Lady Salisbury and Treadwell's Gray Mare. They are reported as winning as often as horses like Sir Peter, Paul Pry and Topgallant. The mares, everybody assumed, were better or worse according to their speed, not according to their sex.

In the late 1830s a remarkable era began in which lovers of fine harness horses developed the suspicion that mares might be a little faster than male horses. In 1838 a five-year-old gray mare, a former inmate of a livery stable, beat a gelding named Sam Patch for an eleven-dollar purse in a race in Babylon, Long Island. She trotted a mile in three minutes. The mare was Lady Suffolk, and the three-minute mile was only a brief foreshadowing of what she could do.

Lady Suffolk raced until the age of twenty-one, starting more than a hundred and fifty times in trotting races throughout the country. Many of them were heat races, which required two or more different miles to claim victory. Not only did she trot hundreds of race miles, but Lady Suffolk trotted thousands of miles between race meets, pulling her racing equipment herself. In 1845, at the age of twelve, Lady Suffolk became the first trotter to go a mile in less than 2:30. Over the next twenty years, Lady Suffolk's world record was broken nineteen times, fourteen times by mares.

Most of those world records can be credited to two great trotting mares, Goldsmith Maid and Flora Temple. They, along with Lady Suffolk, formed a female triumvirate that forever solidified the notion that mares could trot every bit as fast as male horses. The female dominance was not quite so absolute after the retirement of Goldsmith Maid in 1877, but mares held half of the new world mile records set until just after the turn of the century.

Nowadays, world records are divided up according to age and sex, and there is a record recognized for each division. There is still just one overall world record, though, and the occasional trotting mare approaches or even reaches it. In 1984, the three-year-old filly Fancy Crown became co-holder of the overall world record, when she trotted a mile in 1:53 and ⅖ seconds. The record lasted a year before it was broken by a colt. The three-year-old filly Peace Corps trotted in 1:52 and ⅘ seconds in 1989. That was not quite a world record, but it was the second fastest mile ever trotted by any horse.

Other records: Through 1990, the fastest mile ever trotted by a two-year-old was done by a filly. The fastest mile ever trotted by a juvenile on a ⅝-mile track was accomplished by a filly. The fastest ever by an older horse on a ⅝-mile track was trotted by a mare. On the half-mile raceway tracks, the co-fastest overall mile, the fastest

The mare Peace Corps was the most dominant trotting horse in the world between 1989 and 1991. Her sex was not a factor. (Photo credit: USTA)

Miss Easy, at her peak as a two-year-old in 1990, was as fine a pacing filly as harness racing had seen since the days of Fan Hanover a decade before, but even she was unable to compete in open company. (Photo credit: USTA)

three-year-old mile and the fastest older horse mile were all trotted by fillies and mares.

Trotting females are undoubtedly, all else being equal, pretty much as fast as trotting males. But they no longer win the big open races. Twelve fillies have won the Hambletonian, but only one in the past two decades. The Kentucky Futurity, won precisely half of the time by fillies between its beginning in 1893 and 1941, when it took a break for World War II, has been won by fillies only five times since its return to the racing schedule in 1946.

It's hardly surprising. There is a Hambletonian Oaks worth nearly half a million dollars, a Kentucky Futurity Filly Division worth nearly a hundred thousand and many other lucrative, easier filly-only events.

Sometimes a mare is just so good that same-sex races are hardly worth her time and talent. The big strong Peace Corps is such a mare. After a two-year-old season that included a world record, the Kentucky-bred filly was sold for $1.8 million to Sweden. She raced around the world through the age of six, at one point winning twelve straight open races in three different countries. She has no equivalent in the pacing ranks, and probably never will.

Pacing

Trotting may be the natural gait of most horses, but there have almost always been certain horses who employ the same-side movement of the pace. Geoffrey Chaucer mounted some of his Canterbury pilgrims on pacing horses. Paul Revere's mount paced her way to Lexington and Concord. Some hippologists believe they can trace directly a pacing gene back to Friesian horses of the time of Julius Caesar.

Pacing blood found its way into the developing Standardbred breed, and although pacers were greatly outnumbered by trotters on the racetracks of the nineteenth century, it became obvious to everybody who enjoyed harness racing that pacing was the faster gait. Pacing competition became organized more slowly, but by the late nineteenth century the sport was widespread and popular in the United States and Canada.

In the early days there were a few pacing mares equally as good as male horses. In 1844 Aggie Down became the first harness horse of either gait to complete a mile in less than 2:30. In 1855 Pocahontas paced a mile in 2:17 and ½ seconds. That record stood for more than a decade. But that was it for pacing mares and overall world records.

Only one filly has ever won pacing's most prestigious event, the Little Brown Jug. One filly has won the Cane Pace. Two fillies have won the Messenger. No filly has won the richest race of all, the Meadowlands Pace. Female pacers are not, on average, competitive with male pacers.

There are exceptions. In 1990 Miss Easy paced the fastest mile ever by a two-year-old, male or female. The record lasted only a couple of months, but her accomplishment was unique in modern harness racing history. It had people talking about match races with colts and about a full three-year-old campaign in the open division. Neither came to pass, and Miss Easy's experience underlined the fact that the most brilliant of pacing females does best in her own division.

Are Trotters More Competitive?

For more than a hundred years people have been trying to figure out why trotting mares are more competitive than pacers. It may be conformation or it may be genetics. It's probably a combination of several things.

Both trotters and pacers are Standardbreds. There are trotting bloodlines and pacing bloodlines, and one rarely produces an outstanding example of the other. But if you go back enough generations, the ancestry is the same. On the other hand, there are differences in appearance between trotters and pacers. Both groups are becoming finer and more conventionally attractive in appearance; the demands of the auction marketplace have seen to that. But there remains a different look to each group, and an experienced harness racing observer can distinguish a trotter from a pacer even before seeing them move.

It starts with the head. The trotter's head is usually more Thoroughbred-like in appearance, while the pacer's often shows a heavier muzzle and sometimes a roman nose. The head doesn't affect racing ability, but a consistent difference in appearance suggests that substantially different genetic pools are providing the materials for today's trotters and pacers. It's possible that the gene pool for trotters contains some female sex-linked athletic talent.

It's more likely a simple matter of conformation. Trotting is a rear-engine gait, particularly at the high speeds that racing Standardbreds reach. Almost every good trotter has relatively wide hindquarters. The neck doesn't seem to matter a great deal. Fillies are usually most powerful behind.

Top pacers often have modest hindquarters, but they invariably have strong, deep shoulders and a powerful neck. The pacer's parallel gait appears to require the kind of muscles more often found in male horses.

Whatever the reason, the contrast exists. Trotting females are much more competitive—possibly fully equal, given equal opportunity—with males, while pacing females are not. In each gait, the contrast is with colts and stallions, not geldings. As in Thoroughbred racing, the best-bred horses tend to be the best racers, and well-bred horses are not gelded.

Racing Over Fences

Steeplechasing, hurdling, timber racing, point to point—whatever form it takes, racing over fences is a gelding's game. Few mares compete and fewer still succeed at the higher levels of the sport. In Britain and Ireland, where National Hunt racing compares favorably with flat racing in popularity, there are more meets, more races and more opportunities for mares than there are in North America. But even in the British Isles, most big winners are geldings.

There may be a few physical reasons for this, although conformation is not really the key. Otherwise, stallions would do well, and there are even fewer stallions than mares at the top levels. The heavier male neck and head may be a slight advantage in balance over the jumps, particularly the ones that present a drop on the landing side. The slightly heavier male cannon bones probably help maintain soundness, since there is no equine activity that causes more concussion to the forelegs than racing over fences.

Some trainers think mares don't always concentrate as well as geldings, and a lack of concentration is more likely to show up in a 3- or 4-mile race than it is in a 6-furlong sprint. They like to remind people of the 1941 running of the Virginia Gold Cup, one of the most famous trophies in American steeplechasing. A mare named Comedienne, running near the lead, suddenly turned off course, taking the other five leaders with her. All six were disqualified, and the seventh-place finisher took home the trophy.

Comedienne's little joke was an aberration. Most mares perform predictably, according to their running speed and jumping talent. The problem is that unaltered horses, male and female, don't get nearly the opportunity to show off their speed and talent on the steeplechasing course that geldings do.

Steeplechasers are much older than the average flat racehorse. Few even begin training over fences until the age of four or five. They may start in hurdle races or low-fence timber events at that early age, but the steeplechasers who compete in the big-fence, big-money races don't approach their peak until the age of seven or eight.

Horses who race well over fences often raced well on the flat previously. Big-time chasers are fast horses. Even if they weren't winners on the flat—and many of them were—they almost certainly showed some racing talent. A mare older than four who showed racing talent is usually worth more, even in times of fallen markets, in the breeding shed than on the steeplechase course. This is probably the most important reason we see so few mares in the higher levels of racing over fences.

When one is permitted to show her talent, racing fans rejoice. No steeplechaser of modern times was more cherished by fans than the well-bred Irish mare Dawn Run, whose accomplishments would have inspired awe even if she hadn't been a mare in a gelding's sport. Dawn Run jumped well and consistently, but her forte was speed. She was primarily a hurdler, facing lower jumps but faster competition than she would in steeplechasing. She won the Champion Hurdle of England, the Champion Hurdle in France and—to cap a career—the Cheltenham Gold Cup against Europe's top steeplechasers. No horse had ever won all three races.

Dawn Run took off a step too soon on the fifth jump from the finish of the French Champion Hurdle at Auteuil in 1988. She fell heavily, fractured her neck, and died instantly. Her owner had gambled and lost by allowing a good broodmare prospect to show her talent in the sport she was made for. But the rest of the world was far richer for being able to enjoy, although too briefly, Dawn Run's brilliant career.

5

The Show Mare

TODAY'S HORSE SHOW HAS ITS ROOTS IN THE DISTANT PAST, EVEN though the show as a sporting competition is not much more than a century old. There are traces of the Greeks and their mounted Olympic Games in today's horse show, as well as aspects of horse-back circus attractions that became popular in Europe in the 1700s. But the more immediate ancestry dates from the middle of the nineteenth century.

In the days when the horse was almost exclusively a working creature, most public showing of horses was for strictly commercial purposes. Prize money and ribbons were secondary. Stallion own-ers might lead or drive their stud prospects to the local agricultural fair, hoping that the judges would place their stamp of approval on the physical qualities of the animals. More and higher stud fees would follow. Mares were less important commercially, but they were not entirely overlooked. A ribbon to a particularly handsome broodmare would increase the price brought by her offspring and would add luster to the reputation of her own sire. But the stallion remained the focus.

Show wins were only modestly lucrative. For example, the three-year-old stallion winner of New York's Orange County Agricultural Fair of 1853 earned a five-dollar prize for his owner. But the victory permitted the owner to later charge and receive a twenty-five-dollar stud fee for the young stallion's services. The fee, although large for the time, turned out to be one of equine history's great bargains. A few years later, when the first sons and daughters of the colt were broken to harness, their lucky owners discovered that they could trot like the wind. The five-dollar prize winner turned out to be Hambletonian, the founding father of the Standardbred breed.

But that was mostly luck. The majority of the fair prize winners turned out to be nothing of the sort, with no talent to pass on except for their ability to look good standing still. During the nineteenth century, the horse was not a decorative creature, and it didn't take long for the people who frequented the horse shows at the fairs—the would-be buyers and breeders—to put pressure on the organizers to require the contestants to be shown in motion. The potential for usefulness, they thought, could not be demonstrated without movement.

Fair-connected trotting races grew out of this idea, as did driving competitions, comparisons under saddle of hunter prospects and other side-by-side demonstrations of equine performance. Horse owners thinking of buying or using the services of the contestants were now able to better judge what they were getting. There was a bonus: The competitions provided entertainment to people who owned no horses but enjoyed watching them in action. Eventually, enthusiasts organized shows unrelated to agricultural fairs—shows whose entire purpose was to display fine horses in athletic competition.

When performance became the major factor in which horses won or lost a competition, stallions gave up their exclusive rights to predominance in the show ring. Gradually, as showing became popular for its own sake, the potential profit from their horses' breeding qualities became less important as a motivator for owners of show horses. They found that there was plenty of satisfaction simply in winning, and that was something they could do with mares as well as stallions.

The conformation-only competition didn't disappear entirely, of course. Today there are events—but rarely entire shows—devoted to judging horses who do nothing but stand attractively on the end of a lead rope. With the possible exception of the burgeoning miniature horse industry, even the horses in these competitions tend to be judged on the basis of their suitability for athletic performance. Conformation events still usually feature same-sex, same-age participants in the individual classes.

Another remnant of the agricultural-fair horse contests exists today, and it's one that can negatively affect mare owners. Reputations are still developed and stud fees raised when a stallion wins in the show ring. Owners and trainers often find it much more profitable to train and promote stallions than either mares or geldings. Forty or more stud fees a year can come from a popular stallion.

This reality affects the percentage of mares competing at the high levels of some sports. An owner who has a good stallion and a great mare may decide to haul the stallion rather than the mare from show to show, because the stallion will bring more money in the long run. Some judges—often unintentionally—fall into the trap of believing promotion and give extra points to a heavily advertised stallion.

This can happen in any sport where there is an element of subjective decision-making on the part of a judge. A mare owner can't do a great deal about it, except to encourage governing bodies to maintain strict licensing rules for judges and to demand that show managers hire only judges known to be objective.

But in some horse show events, it's obvious who wins. Promotion doesn't help, and prejudice has nothing to do with who performs best. Mares should compete in these sports on an equal footing. But in many of them, they simply don't. Why they don't is usually a function of the nature and requirements of the sport and the attitudes of the people involved in it.

Two-time Olympian and top trainer Michael Matz owes most of his success to stallions and geldings, but in the young German-bred Partitur he thinks he may have a mare with the scope and attitude to succeed in Grand Prix show jumping.

Jumping

Show jumping is the most dramatic of the arena-based horse sports, and it's the one sport where the people sitting in the stands know exactly who is winning. The drama and the simplicity have combined to turn show jumping into the dominant image of modern equine sports. When most people hear the words "horse sports," they think *jumping*.

Mares don't and probably never have competed in equal percentages with male horses in the highest levels of show jumping. They have never been excluded from the sport. As early as 1888, a mare held the world high-jump record. A little mare who stood barely 14½ hands cleared 6 feet 10 inches at Madison Square Garden, and she became an object of adulation in the new and growing sport.

But in the century that followed, mares were a clear minority in top-level competitions. During one season in the early 1980s, fewer than 5 percent of the equine competitors on the major North American Grand Prix circuit were female. The percentage in Europe was probably lower.

This percentage does show signs of increasing. By 1991, about 20 percent of the Top Ten lists—there are several, depending on who is doing the counting—were mares, and more than 10 percent of the dozens of winners of Grand Prix events on the various circuits were mares. But that's still nothing like the 50 percent you might expect if mares were fully equal in the ability to jump a competitive round in an arena.

Does that mean mares are not as good as male horses in stadium jumping? Probably. There are a few physical and mental reasons for this, but there are also economic reasons, as well as reasons resulting from the structure of the sport. On average, mares may not jump quite as well as male horses, but their inferiority is probably much less than the percentage of participation would indicate. For proof, look at the most important jumping awards—gold medals in the Olympic Games.

During the 1950s through the 1980s—the time of the most rapid growth and participation in show jumping around the world—

only two horse-rider combinations were individual and team gold medalists in the Olympics. That happened in 1956 and 1984. Hans Günter Winkler did it in 1956, and Joe Fargis repeated the remarkable accomplishment twenty-eight-years later. Both were mounted on mares. The nearest miss came in 1992, when Dutch rider Piet Raymakers, who won a team gold, failed by .25 fault to win an individual gold. He, too, was mounted on a mare, Ratina Z. It took another mare, the German Classic Touch, to beat her.

Halla

Halla was an international star of the first magnitude, her reputation burning brightly throughout the equestrian world during the 1950s. But her birth came in the darkest of times and places. She was foaled south of Frankfurt, Germany, early in 1944, just as General George Patton's troops were marching into the heartland of Nazi Germany. They passed within a few miles of the stud where she was foaled.

Halla's sire was a German trotting stallion named Oberst, and her dam was a French prize of war called Helene, taken by the German army during their occupation of France. Helene's breeding was unknown, but she appeared to be a refined Thoroughbred type, possibly Anglo-Norman. There was no proof that either parent could jump, but both were athletic horses.

Halla survived the fall of Hitler, and she was entered in steeplechase races as a four- and five-year-old. At 16.3, she was tall enough to handle the biggest courses and fast enough to win, but it was her jumping ability that attracted attention. She was thought to be a three-day-event prospect, and after brief training she shone in cross country and stadium jumping. But Halla, always on her toes, proved unsuitable for the discipline of dressage. The mare's future was, at best, uncertain.

A young three-day-event rider named Hans Günter Winkler got the mount on the slender, fine-necked six-year-old. They placed in several events, but Winkler came to believe that the future for both

Halla and himself lay in the show jumping arena. He was right. They rose quickly through the ranks of international jumping. By the end of 1952 they were the top pair in jumping-crazy Germany. The next year the dark bay Halla earned her niche as a puissance and speed-jumping specialist, an odd combination of talents that suited her on-edge, impetuous nature.

By 1954 she was a specialist at anything that went on in an arena. She won the Men's World Championship for Winkler in Madrid, and then completed a six-win tour of North America. The Stockholm Olympics of 1956 provided a stage for the greatest accomplishment of both Halla's career and Winkler's, when they won the individual gold and the team gold for Germany. In 1960, at the age of sixteen, Halla won a final team gold in the Rome Olympics before her retirement to life as a broodmare.

Halla was everything that some people criticize in show jumping mares—nervous, sometimes difficult and rather light-bodied. But she was also everything that a show jumper should be—consistent, determined and sound. She could have been no better if she had been male.

Touch of Class

The 1973 foal out of the Thoroughbred mare Kluwall did not have a great deal of potential. Kluwall herself, having never earned a penny on the racetrack, was a giveaway. She had shown no discernible racing talent. Besides, she had shaken up her training stable by escaping one day at Pimlico and jumping a chain-link fence. Such behavior is not admired in a racehorse.

In her not particularly well-earned retirement, Kluwall was bred on a free season to a Thoroughbred stallion of modest accomplishment named Yankee Lad. Kluwall produced a pretty bay filly who was later named Stillaspill.

Stillaspill emulated her dam in one way: she started six times, never earning a check. In her final start in 1975, she could have been claimed for $1,500 at Charles Town racetrack in West Virginia. Luckily for her owner, nobody thought she was worth that kind of money.

Although Stillaspill was only slightly over 16 hands and light boned, her athletic, rangy build looked like it could handle fences. She was tried out over fences, but her edgy temperament made her unsuitable for steeplechasing. She was finally sold as a show hunter and renamed Touch of Class.

Maybe it was the name that transformed her. But more likely it was the fact that she was finally introduced to something she was born to do. A huge but flexible stride that made her a little too much for the hunter ring was perfect for the Grand Prix circuit. The boldness and fire that made her too hot for the steeplechase course made her brave enough to challenge jumps that would give pause to 18-handers.

After being bought in 1981 by Olympians Conrad Holmfeld and Joe Fargis and several partners, Touch of Class jumped to a series of Grand Prix and Nations' Cup victories. In August of 1984 she and Fargis qualified for the Olympic Games, held on the grounds of the legendary Santa Anita Park racetrack in southern California. Of the four American riders, only Touch of Class had two clear rounds in the team competition. But the others jumped well enough to join the small bay mare in the gold medal canter.

In the individual competition five days later, Touch of Class jumped three more rounds—two perfect, one with one rail down. She and Fargis won their second gold. No horse had ever jumped so many clear rounds in an Olympic Games. Stillaspill the racehorse wouldn't have qualified for the cheapest claiming race at Santa Anita, but Touch of Class the show jumper honored the famous old place with her presence.

Other Great Jumpers

Other great jumping mares have graced show arenas around the world. Germany thought it was witnessing the second coming of Halla when the Hanoverian mare Simona reached her peak in the early 1970s. The powerful chestnut never quite matched Halla's record, but she did help pick up a team gold medal for Germany in the 1972 Olympics in Munich, just missing a bronze in the individual competition.

Simona won a European championship, a men's World championship and a Nations' Cup with rider Hartwig Steenken. Early in 1974 she was considered to be the most valuable nonracing horse in the world, valued at nearly $200,000, when she was sixteen years old. She retired the following year.

In spite of Simona and Touch of Class, the 1960s through the 1980s were the age of nearly absolute male dominance in show jumping. By the early 1990s that started to change.

Joe Fargis, who knew as well as anybody that a mare could do anything that needed to be done in the jumping ring, developed the Irish-bred mare Mill Pearl into one of the top Grand Prix horses in the world in the late 1980s. By 1991 the twelve-year-old solid chestnut was one of the top three or four horses in the United States and was the leading money winner on the National Grand Prix League circuit. Although of adequate size and power, Mill Pearl's wins were often due to pure speed around a course in a jump-off. Injuries to her rider have compromised her record during the last few years.

Other female winners of important Grand Prix events during the early nineties have included multiple winners Voila T, Serengeti and Silver Skates. Younger winners and near-winners include Italia, Wula, Ramira, Lynsaya, Albonnie and the extremely talented High Heels. These mares are ridden by some of the country's best riders, including Margie Goldstein, Jeffrey Welles and Katie Prudent.

Hunters

Although both are based on jumping, show hunting and show jumping are different sports. Clearing the fences is only part of what the hunter has to do; it's everything to the jumper. The hunter must demonstrate physical suitability to hunting; the jumper can look like a cow if he or she can get over the jumps. The hunter must show even pace; the jumper can gallop, walk or trot, as long as he doesn't incur time faults. The hunter is judged on manners and way of going; the jumper can throw up his head and kick out at jumps, provided he doesn't knock anything down.

It's not that jumping is uncontrolled. Jumpers must put in the precise number of strides that the rider figures they need to reach the perfect takeoff spot, and they must reach and maintain the pace the rider decides will give them the proper momentum. But they don't have to be graceful and they don't have to be well mannered. All they have to do is jump.

Hunters do it all. The jumps are not quite as high for the hunters, but they are high enough to challenge the athleticism of the horses. All in all, the requirements of show hunting are so demanding that a lot of people think that mares are psychologically less suited than geldings for the hunting ring. Many trainers and professional riders shy away from mares for this reason, but the reluctance to use mares at the top levels of hunter competition is disappearing.

In 1991 the American Horse Shows Association awarded nine overall hunter champion titles. Five went to mares, including the two top awards. The overall conformation hunter was the six-year-old Dutch-bred mare Rox Dene, whose perfection in the ring had spectators shaking their heads. The overall working hunter title went to the seven-year-old Thoroughbred mare Bittersweet, who became a national champion each year she competed. Both were models of consistency.

It's clear from this that mares can and do compete at the highest levels of show hunting, but geldings remain dominant in numbers, and most professionals admit to preferring them. In this, they are much like the trainers and riders of jumpers. Nobody would turn down a Mill Pearl or a Bittersweet if she came along, but if they were offered a chance to compete with a mare or a gelding of equal talent, most would pick the gelding. The prejudice is not entirely baseless, although it tends to lessen in direct proportion to the person's experience with a good mare.

Take the case of Thom Pollard, formerly an "A" circuit hunter-jumper trainer, manager of the exclusive Ox Ridge Hunt Club, and now an equestrian educator. He admits to preferring to work with geldings, but he's quick to point out that Aspen Glow, one of the most successful and talented horses he ever trained, was a mare. He believes there are psychological as well as physical reasons to lean toward geldings for show ring jumping, but he also knows from experience that you can develop a fine female jumper in spite of them.

The Jumping Mare's Mind

Thom Pollard is a firm believer in controlling estrus through medication. "With regular veterinary supervision," he adds. "When you spend the kind of money you have to for a good jumper, you want to make sure she can have babies later. We would keep Aspen Glow on the drug through the show season, then give her vacations afterwards." It worked. She competed successfully, then was fertile on retirement.

But Pollard finds mares difficult even apart from estrus. "I don't think their minds tend to lend themselves to training," he says. "In my experience, they sometimes object to the entire training process. With most geldings, when you put your leg on them and squeeze, they go forward. If a mare doesn't like the idea, she may not only not go forward, she may move against the leg or even kick out. She often has too much of a mind of her own."

In some sports, a mind of her own is not only good, it's vital. If a polo pony is not able to make most of its own decisions, it's not going to be much of a player. In a match of experienced players and ponies, the rider relies on the pony to follow the ball and the flow of play. In cutting, the horse has to make its own decisions, since the rider is required to drop his reins during the actual working of the cow. It's no coincidence that these are sports where mares go well beyond being equal to geldings. In jumping, the rider wants response and effort, not decisions.

Still, jumping—particularly big-time stadium jumping—is not done successfully by equine sluggards. "A show jumper has to be aggressive," Pollard says, "and that usually means they're aggressive outside the ring. That aggression, properly channeled, makes for a good performer—one who will want to jump the jump."

Pollard thinks mares might be easier to channel than stallions. "Stallions are so aggressive they might charge right through a jump. Aspen Glow was careful because she was so interested in herself. She was very brave about the jump but she didn't want to get hurt." There is a strong self-protective streak in mares—probably stronger than in stallions or geldings because of the dictates of nature—and this probably helps some mares take extra care over jumps.

Pollard also finds mares are more likely to be unforgiving of a rider's mistakes. Aspen Glow, a superb jumper and well conformed, was not a success in the hunter ring because of a tendency to swish her tail and pin her ears when she became annoyed with her riders' urgings. She moved to jumping, where the occasional signs of annoyance didn't lose her any points. Once she found a rider who rode her the way she expected, she was nearly unbeatable in her class.

Conformation

Mares can jump perfectly well. Some of them can jump with as much beauty and grace as any horse, some of them can jump as high and some of them can jump as wide. Many of them are faster around jump-off courses than male horses of similar quality. But fewer mares than geldings compete and win at the highest levels, and that is caused by more than psychology.

The average male horse who has been bred to jump is slightly more suited physically to modern show jumping than the average mare who has similar conformation and breeding. There are thousands of exceptions. Mill Pearl is far better than the vast majority of male Irish-breds, for example. Good jumpers come in every variety of equine conformation, display every known physical flaw and can look like just about anything. But certain physical characteristics help, and some of them are more likely to be possessed by male than female horses.

"Neck and shoulders have so much to do with the bascule that the horse does in the air," Pollard says. That ability to use the front end to balance the rear in the arc of the jump is often the key to the success of the jump. "A heavier neck helps to balance the horse," Pollard adds. "His head and neck are the balancing agents and critically affect his ability to arc over a fence. A light-necked horse usually can't get around the big courses today."

Male horses have heavier, more muscular necks than similar female horses, and many also have heavier heads. That is a built-in physical advantage in a big Grand Prix course. Jumpers on big courses also need strong, heavy cannon bones, just to stay sound through the repeated impact caused by coming down from a high jump. Male horses have an advantage here, too. A would-be buyer of a jumping mare should look for good neck and substantial bone, but it's wise to remember that both Halla and Touch of Class were slender-necked and light of bone.

Every jumping horse, male or female, should have considerable balance, should demonstrate a smooth stride at the slower gates and should have a stride of considerable length if the owner expects to be competitive in open events. Hocks are extremely important, but it's acceptable for a jumper to have her back legs under her. She may even be cow-hocked, but very few good jumpers are back in the hock. Shoulders are important, with enough angle needed to allow a long stride and enough depth to provide power. These are ideals; there are great jumpers who lack almost every one of these characteristics, but more who have them.

Training the Female Jumper

Many mares seem to want to feel that they are equal participants in their activity, and the controlled nature of both show jumping and hunting sometimes makes them rebel. Many trainers find it

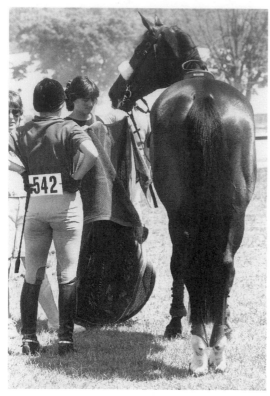

Debbie Dolan and Ramira have already had some success in Grand Prix competition. Ramira, although feminine in the head and neck, has the powerful, deep hip and excellent hindquarters to handle challenging courses.

Ray Texel's young mount Kitty Hawk shows the kind of attitude and concentration necessary in the jumping arena.

worthwhile to be extremely careful with their approach to a mare. "You have to be subtle," Pollard says, "and you have to realize that they may be more sensitive. The fit of the saddle, for example, is going to mean more to a mare than a gelding. They like to know you're being careful. You can't dominate a mare the way you can a gelding. That may be why most trainers like geldings, because you can dominate and program them."

Pollard also finds mares less tolerant of upheaval or even simple change. "I think consistency means more to a mare than a gelding," he says. "They need to be fed at the same time and turned out at the same time. I think they do better with the same groom, as opposed to having somebody different come by every day."

With Aspen Glow, Pollard found consistency to be a problem in one area. "She would fall in love with any gelding who was next to her," he says. "We even had to change the loading order in the van." Training a top mare was a challenge and brought more work. But when asked if he would take another Aspen Glow, he says, "I'd absolutely do it again." Difficulties can be worked out.

Dressage

There are even fewer mares at the top levels of dressage than in open jumping. The 1991 end-of-year list of the best American dressage competitors shows no mares in the top fifteen of the Grand Prix–level horses and only one among the top fifteen of the next highest level, Intermediaire II. The German riders and trainers, who dominate the sport nowadays, appear to be somewhat more enthusiastic about mares than the rest of the dressage world. Late in 1991, reigning European freestyle champion Sven Rothenberger paid a reported $590,000 for an eight-year-old Dutch-bred mare named Bo. She had won the the Dutch National Dressage Championship a few months earlier.

No European dressage enthusiast would have considered criticizing the considerable purchase price on the basis of Bo's sex. After all, a few months later a mare proved herself the best in the world.

Fabienne

A chestnut Westphalian mare burst on the international dressage scene during the winter season of 1991–92. All by herself, Fabienne proved that nothing inherent in being a mare prevents winning at the highest levels of the sport. Young German rider Isabell Werth, who had won the European and German National Championships in 1991 with her trainer's gelding Gigolo, hoped to do as well in 1992 with another gelding, the Hanoverian Weingart. Freestyle music was selected with Weingart in mind, and the program was choreographed for him. But Weingart died late in 1991, and Werth's trainer urged her to challenge the world with a mare.

Using Weingart's music, Fabienne and Werth placed and won in qualifying Grand Prix and freestyles throughout Europe. Fabienne became the only mare to qualify for the World Cup Finals in Sweden in April of 1992. There she showed a huge and enthusiastic crowd that she is one of the few horses in the world able to piaffe perfectly on first asking. The trot in place requires extraordinary physical and mental control, but Fabienne made no mistakes. Near-perfect completion of two nearly as difficult movements, the pirouette and passage, were enough to give Fabienne the Grand Prix, the Freestyle and the overall World Cup title. A twelve-year-old mare stood at the top of the dressage world.

Will Fabienne's remarkable accomplishment give riders and trainers the impetus to look more closely at female dressage prospects and to pay more attention to the ones they have? It's too early to tell, but many competitors have discovered that pleasant personal experiences with a particular mare have caused them to look with more interest at the next mare they are offered.

What Makes a Dressage Prospect?

Strictly speaking, any horse can learn the elements of dressage. The U.S. Dressage Federation describes the purpose of the sport as "the harmonious development of the physique and ability of the horse."

The horse demonstrates its development by showing free and regular paces, ease of movement, impulsion and submission to the rider's wishes. But some horses lack the physical and mental characteristics to do more than get through the basics. Their minds or bodies prevent them from developing truly free paces, impulsion and submission. These horses certainly benefit from dressage training, becoming suppler and more responsive than they would have been without it, but they will never compete successfully at anything but the most preliminary levels of the sport. But the proper characteristics can be found in horses of either sex.

The Mental Characteristics Necessary in Dressage

Sarah Geikie is a dressage competitor and judge who also trains horses and riders for the sport. She never rejects mares because of their sex and currently has several good young prospects in training. But even she admits that both training and competition can be a greater challenge with a mare than with a gelding or even a stallion.

"It's hormones," she says. "Even if they're not in heat when they go to a show, they get excited by the atmosphere and often come into heat, and most mares perform differently when they're in season. Most competition mares are on altrenogest (the primary estrus-controlling drug), but even then they tend to be less consistent in training."

Geikie finds another common mare characteristic incompatible with dressage, particularly in competition. "In dressage, a horse needs to use his body to the maximum so he can show engagement and impulsion, but that has to be combined with total relaxation," she says. "You ask the horse for everything he can give you, but he must do it with complete control and relaxation." Mares, who do so well in the galloping sports, often show a little tension. It doesn't hurt—and often helps—to be tense and on edge in a running sport, but it's deadly to the scores in dressage.

Geikie says the most important mental characteristic for dressage training is something that *can* be found in mares. "I really stress

To Sarah Geikie, temperament is everything. The Thoroughbred mare Caplet is so willing that Geikie thinks she can be made into a good dressage performer. A deep, well-angled shoulder helps, too.

The Anglo-Trakhener Christabel has been in dressage training for less than two weeks here, but her intelligence and willingness have already made her a fine prospect. She is neither as tall nor as long-necked as Sarah Geikie might have wanted, but she is learning to use her good body angles to produce an attractive neck position and a big-horse stride.

temperament," she says. "Without it, no matter how talented the horse is, you'll never get through to them." By temperament, she means willingness and good nature. For her own safety and peace of mind, she does not like to deal with dangerous and difficult animals. She describes the mares she has accepted for training varyingly as having a "lovely attitude," "sweet" and "one of the nicest horses I've ever had." The mares return the affection and have been extremely willing to put up with the mental and physical challenges of dressage.

Geikie believes that most horses can learn to behave well. "If you have the attitude that he or she will develop and that it's essentially a good horse, it will probably become a good horse. If you take the opposite approach, the opposite tends to happen."

Physical Requirements of Dressage

Geikie points out that conformation is not supposed to matter in dressage. She says she and most other judges are conscientious about not grading a horse down because of its looks. "You simply cannot judge the horse in the dressage ring on the basis of conformation," she says. "You judge their way of going and how the horses look relative to their way of going."

But she admits that some conformational characteristics lead to limitations. "Some conformation problems inhibit a horse's ability to perform certain movements," she says. "Horses that are built very straight through the hip angle and gaskin, like some Thoroughbreds, may never have the kind of use of the joints it will need for a high level of flexion and collection. You must have a good angle there."

A deep hip with power enough to transfer weight from the forehand—as well as to perform the extremely difficult movements like piaffe and passage—can be found in either sex, as can a deep shoulder with good angle for a big stride, good length of the croup for range of motion and adequate flexion in the hocks. But dressage also requires a powerful neck to maintain the shape so admired in the dressage ring. Geikie says that, while male horses might seem to have a hormonal advantage in the ability to put on muscle in the neck, she's convinced that mares can put on muscle in that region as well.

"From my experience, the strong look of the neck comes with training," she says. "Correct training in head and body placement develops the right muscles in the neck. When a horse goes correctly forward with its hind legs and has learned to relax and use its back, the rider is able to maintain the correct shape for enough time so the horse gets strong in the back. As you develop the back, you get that neck."

Male horses may have one physical advantage that is impossible to overcome. They tend to have larger, heavier bone, and the bone of the joint is important in dressage. "You want horses who have well-formed large joints," Geikie says, "although they can't be excessive." But many mares do have adequate joint size for their body weight, and they should be able to handle the stress on their joints that the most difficult dressage movements cause.

The Warmblood Domination and the Mare

International dressage and show jumping have been taken over by warmbloods. A dozen or more breeds are involved in this takeover, most of them developed out of centuries or just a few decades of crossing European working horses with hot-blooded Thoroughbreds, mostly from Britain.

The result proved to be horses ideally suited for show ring work. They retain the athleticism and much of the competitiveness of the Thoroughbred, but these attributes are contained in a taller, more muscular and generally calmer package. Both dressage and jumping have come to take advantage of the physical characteristics of the warmbloods. The dressage world wants a powerful body rounded into a shape that's much easier to obtain from a warmblood than from the other athletic breeds. The jumping world has encouraged the design of enormous Grand Prix courses with jumps of such width and height that only big, muscular and strong-boned horses can easily navigate them. There are exceptions, but the average successful Grand Prix horse is a big and powerful animal.

At the same time, economics pushed the sound and athletic young Thoroughbred out of the price range of most show competitions. Until the Thoroughbred market collapsed in the late 1980s, any Thoroughbred with physical potential was worth far more as a racing prospect than as a show prospect. If it proved its athleticism on the racetrack, it was hurried off to stud. Many of the racetrack failures were not athletic enough for the show ring either. So good Thoroughbreds were not as easily available to dressage or jumping competitors or for breeding purposes at a reasonable price.

This economic reality is important in trying to understand the changing role of mares in the show ring, at least in North America. There are good mares and good male horses in every breed and type, but the ideal characteristics of some breeds can be more closely correlated with the common characteristics of one sex or the other. For example, Quarter Horses need to be heavy in the hindquarters but relatively light in front to get away quickly, stop suddenly and turn on the hocks. That's a mare's conformation, and mares are on a par with colts in most Quarter Horse sports. (See Chapter 7, "The Western Mare," for more on this subject.)

Thoroughbreds need to be relatively light of body and not too heavy in the neck, at least while they are in training. A touch of nervousness is usually no problem. Mares qualify in all categories.

Warmbloods, on the other hand, are supposed to be heavily boned, heavily muscled and somewhat phlegmatic. These are not mare characteristics, although the warmblood breeds produce mares who possess them to a certain extent. It may be that warmblood breeds are not "mare breeds" as the Thoroughbred and Quarter Horse breeds are.

Alois Podhajsky, one of the most celebrated proponents of modern dressage, noticed this decades ago. As director of the Spanish Riding School in Vienna, he loved his Lippizaners. As a dressage competitor and trainer, he loved mares. But even he acknowledged that Lippizaner mares were not particularly good in dressage. Many of his favorite mounts from his days before Vienna and while at the Spanish Riding School were mares, but almost all were Thorough-bred or Thoroughbred crosses.

But warmbloods are so suited to the modern dressage and jump-ing arenas that even the most devoted lover of mares would be foolish to avoid them. Fabienne is a warmblood, as are Mill Pearl and Silver Skates. But the good jumping mares in particular tend to be Thoroughbred-type warmbloods or Thoroughbred crosses. In searching for a mare who fits the ideal physical type for the particular sport, it's probably unwise to choose a mare that looks too male. Delicate and feminine might not be good, but massive may not be right for a mare either. A good mare type in a body suited to the sport should be the goal.

We may be seeing more mares in competition during the 1990s and beyond because good Thoroughbreds are becoming more avail-able for purchase and breeding. Prices have shrunk for both young horses and stud fees, and show ring people again have a chance to compete with the racing market. An athletic mare—even a modestly successful one—who might have been hurried off to the breeding shed ten years ago could now be equally valuable as a dressage or jumping prospect.

Combined Training

Combined training, also called horse trials or three-day eventing, consists of competition in three equine sports in which mares usu-ally tend not to excel at the highest levels—steeplechase racing in the form of a cross-country run, dressage and stadium jumping. Nevertheless, mares compete and win in higher percentages in eventing than they do in any of those individual sports, at least in North America. A recent year featured thirty-nine female winners of events registered by the United States Combined Training Asso-ciation at the preliminary level or above. They represented nearly 14 percent of all winners. None was a top ten competitor, but the list included several very young mares of great promise, a few of whom were multiple winners against male competitors.

The fact that warmbloods do not and cannot dominate eventing may help explain the slightly better overall performance of mares in this sport as compared to Grand Prix jumping and dressage. The best eventers are Thoroughbred, mostly Thoroughbred or half Thoroughbred. Rarely do other breeds have the speed and stamina to compete satisfactorily in the cross-country phase, which accounts for three-quarters of the total points. It's no surprise that all but a handful of the winning mares had a substantial dose of Thoroughbred blood.

Another factor that contributes to the competitiveness of mares is the lower level of demands in the show jumping and dressage phases of the three-day event. Eventers are not asked to leap 6-foot fences with an equally demanding spread, as Grand Prix jumpers are expected to do. In dressage, they do not have to attempt the piaffe, which requires so much pure muscular strength. The cross-country phase counts most, and the speed and agility that come easily to a good athletic mare come into play in this section.

Occasionally, a mare—even a warmblood mare—will develop into a combined training competitor who can compete with anybody. German rider Herbert Blocker rode his thirteen-year-old Hoisteiner Feine Dame to an individual silver and a team bronze in the 1992 Olympic games.

Nevertheless, the best eventers are not mares and probably never will be. A top eventer must be fast, and a fast Thoroughbred mare will go to the breeding farm rather than on the combined training circuit. A Thoroughbred dam of fast offspring will not be bred to a nonracing stallion, and a fast Thoroughbred stallion will be too expensive for the owner of a sporting rather than racing mare. The recent price collapse in the Thoroughbred market has made some reasonably fast mares available for something other than breeding, but the very best and most promising will be kept racing or in racing production.

In-Hand Showing

Most horses shown in-hand appear in same-sex, same-age classes, so that judges can compare individuals, not characteristics that result from sex. But the two sexes do compete for Grand Champion titles, where the individual class winners are compared, and in pleasure classes, where the order of finish is based on appearance rather than performance.

Some judges clearly prefer the look of a stallion. Whether it's the crested neck or the heavier muscle or the bigger bone, there is something in the unaltered male that attracts the eye of certain judges. Others like a more refined and graceful look, and such judges may prefer a mare. In most breeds shown primarily for appearance, geldings seldom win against strong competition. The presence, style and musculature of the stallion and the grace of the mare make it difficult for geldings to compete in open conformation classes.

Some handlers believe that certain grooming techniques will help create a more competitive appearance in a mare when she's competing before a judge who likes a male look. They will thin her tail a little to make her hindquarters look even more powerful. They may trim her bridle path a little lower on the neck to make the neck look wider, or they may use lotions to make her mane look fuller. A book on show grooming will tell you how to enhance a horse's appearance.

Most handlers don't bother to read books, however. They focus their competition on other mares, and don't spend a lot of time worrying about judicial prejudice.

6

The Polo Mare

IN NO OTHER EQUESTRIAN SPORT DO SO MANY MARES PERFORM SO WELL at the highest levels of competition as they do in polo. Mares can and sometimes do participate at least equally against male horses in Quarter Horse racing and cutting. If given the opportunity, they probably could do the same in trotting and sprint-distance Thoroughbred racing. In polo, "probably" and "could" are not involved, and "equal" isn't in question. High-goal, outdoor polo, which features the best teams and players, is a mare's game. This is true even though polo requires the greatest level of equine courage and aggression of any of the horse sports.

A few years ago I watched a championship match of the Saratoga Polo Association, featuring two of the three or four best polo teams in the United States. The string of one team consisted of twenty-three mares and one gelding; the other featured seventeen mares. You might find the percentages to be different with other teams, but chances are excellent that they won't be much different, at least until you drop down to the club or intercollegiate level. Even then, you are likely to find that many of the most skilled ponies are female, perhaps like the University of Connecticut's talented Argen-

Modern polo is a mare's game. All but one of the horses on the field at the start of this high-goal match at the prestigious Greenwich Polo Club are mares. And that includes the referees' mounts.

tine-bred Ikura, who was culled from a professional string because of soundness problems. Her talent was never in question.

We don't know if this ancient sport has always been the domain of mares. Polo is not the same game it was when it arrived in North America late in the nineteenth century, and it's far from the same game played during the earliest days of the sport. The most diligent historian can't state with absolute certainty where and when polo began, much less what kind of horses were used.

Some say that ancient Tibetan hunters originated polo, modeling it on their habit of chasing muskrats on horseback, brandishing clubs to move the hapless little animals around fields and forests. According to this theory, the word "polo" derives from the Tibetan word *pulu*, the willow root from which the game ball was carved.

Still others point to the fact that the first written references to the sport came from farther west. Alexander the Great and King Darius of Persia exchanged letters and gifts for several years prior to 333 B.C. Among the gifts was a polo mallet presented to Alexander by Darius. Alexander dispatched a polite thank-you note to Darius but invaded his kingdom anyway.

Although polo failed as a war-prevention device, the Alexander-Darius letters do suggest that the game was widely played nearly 2,500 years ago. The Persian wood known as *palas* provided the balls for their game, and *polo* may have derived from that word.

But whether polo was first played (and named) in Persia or Tibet, we don't know much about the sex of the horses who played the early game. The Greeks and some of the Eastern peoples used and appreciated mares for both battle and sport, and we can guess that they used their mares in the new game. We do know that they used a lot of horses. Records and art from the days of Darius tell us that a hundred or more mounted players were involved in individual matches. We also know, from the same sources, that the horses were very small—true ponies at this point in polo's history. Over the centuries, the size of the teams shrank to a dozen or so players, and the size of the animals remained small.

Polo was discovered by Europeans in the mid-nineteenth century. Horse-loving British cavalry officers looking for entertainment while stationed in the far reaches of the British Empire, came upon matches in Pakistan and India. They were instantly captivated by the speed and controlled violence of the sport. In 1859 British officers founded the first polo club in India, and ten years later they brought their new game home.

First with nine players to a side, then seven, then five, the game changed and developed. The British set the height limit on ponies at 14 hands, somewhat larger than the 13 to 13.2 that the Indian ponies averaged. The 14-hand restriction was retained when the game arrived in North America in 1876.

New York *Herald* publisher James Gordon Bennett was the founding father of American polo. He imported balls, mallets and rules from England, and he brought boxcar loads of Texas cowponies to sell to would-be players in New York. Most of these ponies were geldings. They were bought and sold cheaply and were not greatly valued as individuals, but the game continued to evolve and the role of the pony changed.

In 1881 the number of players per side was reduced to four. The outdoor field was standardized, where possible, at 300 by 150 yards. The field of play was and is enormous—three times the length of a football field. Speed became vital in a polo pony at the same time that players became more skilled in both performance and training their mounts.

By the time the twentieth century dawned, so did the recognition that the pony made up most of the difference between winning and losing in polo. Individual ponies became known, even famous: Jacobs, Red Angel, Fireball, to name but a few. These were mostly geldings, but as the game opened further and became even faster, mares began to emerge. A specific type of pony was needed, one with speed as well as endurance, good hindquarters for getaway power, but a streamlined body for stamina. The 14-hand height limitation was eliminated just after World War I to accommodate the faster, stronger horses that the new game demanded.

Thoroughbred blood was needed and added to the Quarter-type stock that dominated in the early years of the American game. By the late 1920s, American polo was as good as any in the world, and

As soon as pure speed of foot became the primary factor in top-level polo, mares galloped to the forefront.

Nobody would claim that this mare has ideal equine conformation, with her thin, almost ewe neck and her light body. But she's just fine for a polo pony. She has just completed a successful chukker in a high-goal match between two of the country's best teams.

the mare had become a mainstay of the game. The game suited her physical and mental makeup.

The horse and rider combination reached its peak with Tommy Hitchcock, one of the greatest players ever to ride onto a polo field. His favorite mount was a small, fast mare named Roxanna. She hailed from San Angelo, Texas, and was of Quarter Horse type, although a good dose of Thoroughbred blood was probably mixed in to give her the stamina she needed for six-chukker matches. Hitchcock came from one of the East Coast's most social and sporting families, and he took advantage of his opportunities to make himself into America's most famous polo player.

Hitchcock, on Roxanna whenever possible, led American teams to highly publicized victories in international competition during the late 1920s. It is from this era that we can begin to trace the growing importance of mares as top-level polo mounts. Trophies, whether on display in museums or in private homes, are engraved with names of the ponies as well as the players from the winning teams. On some, the equine names are almost all those of females.

Hitchcock, whose second love after polo was aviation, volunteered for the Army Air Corps at the start of World War II. His death in a plane crash in 1944 marked the end of the already declining Golden Age of American polo. The game was still played after the war, but the publicity—and the international victories—disappeared. Argentina became the dominant power in international polo.

The American game reemerged during the late 1960s, with new polo clubs, tournaments and rivalries being developed. At the highest levels of play, polo remains much the same game as it was during the Golden Age between the two World Wars. But the base has expanded.

Arena polo, played both indoors and out, features a smaller playing field, shorter matches and one less player on each side. That means fewer ponies and less acreage are required. So the cost to play arena polo—particularly the outdoor variety—is substantially lower than for traditional polo. The reduced cost has led to a rapid growth in the number of club polo teams and intercollegiate squads.

The handicap system, in which each player on a side receives a rating from zero goals (for unskilled players) to ten (for the best), provides for better competition. The teams with low-goal players receive a head start in goals equal to their deficiency in total handicap. Some leagues prohibit high-goal players altogether. The ponies are not rated, which is probably a pity, since a beginner aboard a great pony can often outplay an experienced player aboard a poor one.

Arena polo emphasizes slightly different equine characteristics than does traditional outdoor polo. Most players and coaches insist that a good pony will be good on a big field or small one. That's true, but it doesn't necessarily go both ways. A good traditional pony will play well in an arena, but a good arena pony may not be able to carry its talent outdoors because of a lack of speed and stamina. This is important in any discussion of mares in polo, because the percentage of mares differs between the two forms of the game.

Nobody keeps statistics on the sex of the ponies involved in particular matches or leagues, but this is a fact: Geldings are more likely to be found playing arena polo than the high-goal outdoor game. Mares still make up a substantial percentage of arena ponies, but they tend not to dominate the indoor game quite as much as they they do the outdoor version.

Admirers of polo-playing mares might claim that is because most arena teams—universities, clubs and the like—can't afford to buy the best ponies around. They take what they can get, and what they get is the less skilled and valuable pony, often a gelding. There are physical reasons why mares do so well in polo in general, and in full-field polo in particular.

Conformation

Polo ponies are actually horses who, nowadays, rarely stand less than 15 hands or more than 15.3. They must be athletic and they must have speed, but apart from that, some extremely unprepossessing physical specimens can make good polo ponies. Dr. James

The ability to stop and turn quickly—which comes more easily to horses with the typical mare combination of light body weight and wide hindquarters—is important to a successful polo pony.

The mare in the foreground shows excellent polo pony conformation—a light, almost thin body and good muscular hindquarters.

Dinger, an associate professor of animal science at the University of Connecticut who coaches the university's varsity polo teams, says good looks and skill don't necessarily go hand in hand.

"We seem to have a lot of good horses who are ewe-necked," Dr. Dinger says. "You just don't see many thick-necked horses who play good polo. It's a question of agility—they have to be able to turn very quickly at speed." The burden of a large neck probably prevents some otherwise athletic geldings from becoming skilled polo ponies. The fact that mares are usually lighter in the neck probably gives them a distinct advantage.

Extra body weight can also be a problem for a polo pony. "You want the pony to be slim," says Dr. Dinger. "Particularly outdoors, you're not too concerned with substance. You're concerned with speed. It's everything."

But a different kind of horse can prosper in the arena, and this helps explain why geldings become more competitive indoors. "The arena pony has to be a little more like a football player," according to Dr. Dinger. "Speed is not as important indoors. It's nice to have, but the arena is so small that a horse who's a little slow but solid can get on the ball and nobody can push him off it." Outdoors, that same horse might never get on the ball in the first place because somebody else beat him to it in the mad dash downfield.

Wide hindquarters for short turns and quick starts are necessary for all kinds of polo, and mares tend to have a slight advantage here. Other physical characteristics of the ideal polo pony can be found in either mares or geldings: good withers to prevent the saddle from slipping forward, a short back for soundness and agility, short but relatively straight pasterns for quick turns on the hindquarters.

The Mental Side

The psychological requirements of polo might seem to favor male horses, but the fact that mares do so well demonstrates yet again the dangers of superimposing human assumptions on horses. Polo is not a "feminine" sport by human standards.

"A polo pony has to be aggressive," Dr. Dinger explains. "They have to be willing to run into dangerous situations." They can't be afraid of pushing, bumping or running into horses or barriers. Minor injuries are an everyday occurrence, and serious injuries happen to almost every pony who plays for any length of time. A timid horse has no chance to play well. Why do mares take so to the game? It's impossible to claim that female horses are naturally more aggressive than male horses.

Dr. Dinger feels the explanation lies in the kind of aggression required in polo. "While horses have to be aggressive, they have to learn not to retaliate. They have to put up with physical abuse from the other horses and to accept contact from them. That can be difficult. Normally, horses are just like people. There's a space they respect. In polo, the horse has to learn that they can bump and be bumped, push and be pushed out of the way, but that they're not allowed to retaliate."

Some horses find that difficult to learn, and it's possible that some male horses find it a little more difficult. Females are somewhat more inclined to kick than bite in retaliation, while males will do both. The majority of biters, though, are male. "Horses who kick can be trained not to do it," Dr. Dinger says, "but when we find one who bites, he has to be eliminated from the program."

It's difficult to predict in advance of training which horse will have the kind of controlled aggression necessary for success in polo. Some experts think that the great polo-playing mares would all turn out to be alpha mares if they were in herds of their own. Dr. Dinger thinks otherwise.

"You would think that the alpha horse—the horse at the top of the peck order—would be good, but I've found even some of those horses don't like to bump and go right into a play," he says. "Sometimes horses that seem shy around the feed tub, the ones that are lower in the pecking order, do very well. They'll charge right in there."

While courage and aggression are important for success, another mental characteristic is more important for safety. The polo pony has to be consistent, and most players find this no more or less present in mares or geldings. It's a factor of personality, not sex.

"They must be dependable," Dr. Dinger believes. "When you're leaning down to make a shot and the horse turns to go another way, you can kill yourself." With trustworthiness and consistency so important, shouldn't estrus be a problem?

In polo, as in the other galloping sports, being in heat doesn't seem to make a mare perform less well. "Once the game gets going and once you're riding them hard enough, they just don't have a chance to do anything. It may be noticeable in a show ring, but when they're running full speed they don't have time to think about it." As for regulating estrus with medication, Dr. Dinger adds, "To the best of my knowledge, nobody in polo does it. It's not necessary. We treat our mares like our geldings." Estrus may affect a mare while she's waiting during her off-chukker, and she may get a little impatient during shipping, but she's unlikely to show much evidence of it during play.

Training

The physical demands of the sport being so great, few horses are trained for polo before the age of four or five. Some come to polo from other sports—particularly the racetrack—and others are acquired by players or trainers as unbroken or green-broke young adults. In most breeds, mares do mature a little earlier than male horses, both mentally and physically, and this may give mares a slight early advantage in training.

Basic training for polo is nearly identical to that required for any horse sport—or for pleasure riding. An unbroken horse must be made accustomed to handling, tack, a mouthing bit of some kind and then a snaffle. She will probably be lunged before being ridden. After she gets used to being ridden, a trainer will school her exclusively on the flat. The horse will spend weeks, even months, learning to walk, trot, and canter on cue before anything related to polo is introduced.

University of Connecticut polo captain Christian Fox begins shot-taking training with a new mare, first at the trot, then at the canter and gallop.

Fox begins the introduction of the mallet to a mare in training. She accepts it without fear.

There are two differences between early training for polo and early training for other English riding sports. First, the polo pony must learn to turn on a neck rein cue rather than yield to pressure on one side or other of the bit. This is important, since the polo player carries the reins in one hand and would almost never have time to differentiate between reins. Fortunately, most horses quickly learn the object of neck reining—to turn in the opposite direction from the side of the neck on which it feels the weight of the reins.

A horse who has been previously taught traditional turns will usually learn to neck rein quickly, too. The two methods can be combined, with a pull on the bit and weight against the neck at the same time, until the horse learns to respond to one without the other.

Use of the correct lead at the canter and gallop is important in all performance sports, but it's absolutely vital in polo. Early training of a pony requires hours of instruction in striking off on the correct lead as well as changing leads at the gallop. More than in any other sport, the horse in polo must learn to pick the correct lead and to change leads on its own. During play, the rider has so little time to give aids that a horse who needs repeated cues will not be an effective polo pony.

Many trainers in various equine sports are convinced that mares learn more quickly than male horses do, possibly because they are particularly responsive to external stimuli. If this is true, then mares may learn these vital basic polo lessons more quickly and more thoroughly, and that fact may contribute to their apparent overall higher level of skill.

Polo trainers like to find out before devoting too much time to training if the pony prospect is going to have any trouble accepting the presence of mallet or ball. Dr. Dinger says, "The mallet doesn't bother most horses, but you've got to learn fairly early if the horse is going to put up with it." A trainer will carry a mallet without taking shots, tap his horse lightly with it, and wave it within the animal's view to test reactions. Most trainers recognize no sex differences in reaction to the mallet. Early training to accept shots is done at the walk and trot rather than at the canter. Speed comes later.

Good ponies usually follow the ball during the flow of play. "The rider is supposed to guide them," Dr. Dinger says, "but after ponies have played for a while, they learn to go after the ball themselves. The player has to be ready when he's on an experienced pony, because sometimes the horse will go after the ball and leave the rider behind."

Both mares and geldings will learn to follow the ball, but many mares of various breeds seem to have an extra inclination to follow movement. Some western trainers believe this tendency helps explain why mares do particularly well in livestock events. It's possible that mares perform well in polo at least in part because they like to follow moving objects.

We can only speculate why this may be true. Perhaps it's because normal equine social structure has mares happily following other mares, or perhaps it's related to the urge to keep track of their foals. Or perhaps mares are no more likely than geldings to follow a polo ball. But something has to explain why mares are so good at polo, and the inclination to follow could well be part of it. However, conformation and body weight are part of it, too. All in all, the mare makes a package well suited to the game of polo.

7

The Western Mare

IF YOU ASK ALMOST ANYONE IN THE WORLD TO DRAW A PICTURE OF A
typical American horse, chances are you'll get a sketch of an animal
who would look very much at home under a stock saddle. You
might even get a nice picture of the saddle.

Nowadays, at least in terms of horses, "western" refers to use
rather than geography, but both image and use grew out of the
history of a particular time and place. From the moment when
the soldiers of Hernando Cortés led sixteen Cuban-Spanish horses
ashore in Vera Cruz, Mexico, to the time when the motor vehicle
took over most of the heavy work on cattle and sheep ranches, the
horse was an integral part of the development of the western half
of the North American continent.

The image was honed and the legend created in practical work.
Today we recreate the traditional work in stylized form in horse
shows, rodeos and short track racing. Ironically, mares tend to play
a bigger role in the modern western horse world than they did in
the historic one.

Two separate paths led to the creation of today's western horse.
These paths arrived in the West from somewhat different sources,

sometimes ran parallel, sometimes diverged and ultimately came together. One was taken by the Indian peoples of the West, whose lives were changed forever when the Spanish conquistadores reintroduced the horse to the Western Hemisphere. The other was occupied by the European settlers of the West, whose needs were different from those of Native Americans, but who ended up with very similar horses nonetheless.

The Indian Horse

Indian tribes of the American Southwest began acquiring horses in large numbers during the early years of the seventeenth century, buying, trading or stealing them from Spanish outposts. The acquisition continued in earnest during the eighteenth century, and many tribes owned enough horses by the late 1700s to begin trading them back to the Spanish, as well as to French and English settlers willing to go West to get them.

The Indian horses were primarily descendants of Spanish animals, and the ancestors of the Spanish horses were largely of Arab and Moorish origin. As the years passed, some horses of northern European ancestry were added to the equine melting pot. Whatever the source, all the surviving horses adapted to the reality of life in the Southwest, and their descendants managed to get by with limited food and water, negligible shelter and plenty of work. Horses were primarily used for transportation, hunting and war. The more horses, the richer and more mobile the tribe.

There is little evidence that the southwestern Indians had any particular respect or concern for mares, except as general breeding stock. Most tribes felt, as the Spaniards did, that men should ride stallions. But as the horse culture spread north through the Great Plains, some tribes paid closer attention to mares.

The Shoshone, known far beyond their southern Idaho homeland for breeding fine horses, prized mares and cared for them well. When the Lewis and Clark expedition received horses from the Shoshone early in the nineteenth century, they were given only stallions. After the explorers found the stallions troublesome, they asked for mares or geldings. The Shoshone refused them mares. The Indians did agree to show the explorers their quick, safe method of gelding, but didn't give up any of their treasured mares. It was a wise move, since Lewis and Clark were forced to eat most of their horses along the trail.

Trading with settlers became common during the middle of the nineteenth century, at least among the large tribes with horses to spare. But most tribes would trade only stallions, geldings and the occasional older, poor-quality mare. The Indians fully understood the value of a good mare, both for work and breeding. They also understood the value of the alpha mare—the chosen leader of a particular horse herd. Many tribes learned that they could turn their herds out to nearby pasture, then bring them all in simply by sending out one young boy to catch and lead in the alpha.

The greatest of the horse-breeding tribes was also the greatest admirer of mares. The Nez Percé, developers of the magnificent Appaloosa, understood the principles of selecting mares as well as stallions for genetic traits. They practiced the highest level of broodmare care, using but not abusing their in-foal mares, feeding them carefully and valuing them as equal if not superior contributors to the qualities of the foals.

Chief Joseph, the Nez Percé leader who surrendered to the U.S. Army in 1877, was forced to give up his 1,100-head breeding herd that consisted largely of mares. In later years, Chief Joseph often spoke sadly of his horses, regretting their loss nearly as much as he mourned his people's exile to a distant reservation.

The Settlers' Horses

The earliest European settlers brought a different mix of equine genes to the West. Some horses of Spanish ancestry were among their stock, but heavier harness animals and English Thoroughbreds also made the trek westward. Some of these horses found their way to Indian herds, and settlers acquired many Indian horses through purchase or capture. As the decades passed, both the Plains Indians and the settlers, particularly those who turned to cattle ranching,

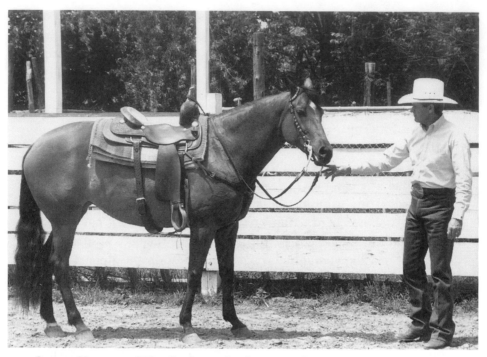

Quarter Horse mare Dillon Spy has cutting horses, race horses and reining horses in her immediate pedigree. She possesses conformation characteristics that would be useful for almost all western sports—deep hip, relatively short neck, short but substantial cannon bone. She's a cutting horse herself, and more than useful.

found themselves with a remarkably similar kind of horse. The typical western horse became a small, quick, agile animal who could live on poor grazing, who had the strong feet and light frame that let it work hard without breaking down and who had a temperament that suited livestock work and permitted easy handling by people. That was what was needed, and that is what people got, either through carefully planned selective breeding or by just keeping and breeding what worked.

Today, although some cow ponies still work cattle, we use most western horses for leisure or for idealized versions of what they used to do. Horse feed comes in by truck, so we don't need to make our horses get by on poor grazing. We have educated farriers and skilled veterinarians, so our horses don't need to rely on only their genes for health. But the work they do creates conformational and psychological requirements similar to those of the old-time Indian horse or cow pony.

If you want a horse that wins in cutting competition, it had better be agile—not too heavy in front, wide enough behind for instant starts and pivots, and with an innate ability to understand and match the moves of other, smaller animals. If you want a horse for steer wrestling, it had better be alert, quick out of the gate, willing to chase down another animal and responsive to the rider but capable of making many of its own decisions.

Given those descriptions, it's not surprising that the modern western competition horse is as likely to be female as male. The percentage of mares to geldings and stallions varies from event to event, but the physical and mental characteristics of mares are ideally suited to much western competition. Many working cowboys preferred to use geldings, since they wanted stock whose attitudes were consistent regardless of the season and who wouldn't spend so much time developing social structure when turned out to pasture. But today's competition cowboy wants stock that wins, and that stock often turns out to be female.

The "Female" Breeds

The breeds that dominate western performance events are often breeds in which characteristics typical of mares are admired as the ideal for the breed as a whole. A good Quarter Horse is supposed to be wide in the hindquarters, flexible in the neck and shoulders and strong but not excessively heavy of bone. Appaloosas and stock-type Paints and Pintos should have these characteristics, too.

Too much weight in the neck and jaw—which mares rarely have—is considered a detriment to flexibility and agility. Muscular necks are important, but until the infusion of Thoroughbred blood changed the western horse outline, even stallions rarely had arched, crested necks in the stock breeds.

A trend to breed and feed for huge muscles and small feet to create the image of masculine power did appear a few years ago. But that trend, with its concurrent increase in navicular disease, unsoundness and inflexibility, seems to be waning. Some conformation judges still like bulging muscles, but in most events where action rather than appearance counts and where winning is not subjective, a good mare conformation is nearly ideal.

Most western performance events are at least a hundred years old, and they certainly weren't designed to take advantage of the particular qualities possessed by mares. Nor were the people who tried to breed competitors for these events hoping in particular to breed good mares.

But in the process of breeding for the conformation and behavior they needed for many of the events, people found themselves intensifying the characteristics that female horses were inclined to have anyway. The differences aren't great—just a little less weight up front, just a little more width in the hips, just a little more inclination to boss a small animal around—but they were enough to make people overlook both estrus and prejudice and use mares fully and well in many western events.

The Mare and "Cow"

In western performance events, "cow" means something other than a four-legged bovine creature. It's a characteristic possessed by a few lucky horses, most often Quarter Horses, but sometimes horses of other breeds. It's a quality that is as likely—possibly more likely—to appear in a mare as in a male horse. If the sport needs "cow," you'll find plenty of mares competing and winning.

"Cow sense" is probably a more accurate term for the characteristic that makes a horse willing and eager to chase, separate or challenge a cow or calf. Almost any horse can be taught to work with livestock, but only a few have an inborn enthusiasm for the activity. Many equine historians believe that the tendency is most common in Quarter Horses because their ancestors included Spanish horses bred specially to work livestock. This may be true, but it doesn't quite explain why some modern Quarter Horses have it and others don't. Cutting horse breeders have succeeded in increasing the percentage of foals capable of succeeding at cutting, but it's very difficult to figure how much of the animal's success is due to cow sense and how much is due to athletic ability.

Competitors in the sports that require "cow" consider it on a par with the physical characteristics that suit the individual events. At the highest levels, a horse needs both the physical ability and cow sense to succeed. One won't work without the other.

Western riders and trainers vary in their eagerness to use mares in competition, but most agree that many of the horses who have a good dose of "cow" are female. In some cattle competitions, such as cutting futurities, more mares than geldings or stallions may participate. In the events with slightly different physical requirements, such as roping, geldings may make up more than half the participants. In still others, such as reining events, the percentage may be about equal.

But if cow sense were the only requirement, mares might dominate. Some experts think that "cow" represents a kind of aggression or bullying on the part of the horse, who wants to prove his authority over the smaller animal. Others—often those who use mares—see "cow" as nothing more than an extension of the horse's desire to supervise the calf or cow, much as a mare might supervise a foal. The obvious desire for control, they believe, is more to assure protection than to cause harm. Only the horses know which interpretation is right, but the fact that mares seem to have so much cow sense might give a little weight to the calf-as-substitute-foal argument.

The cattle-oriented events usually take place within rodeos or in competitions exclusive to the individual event, not at horse shows. Shows featuring hundreds of horses in dozens of divisions rarely have room for even a modest herd of cattle. Consequently, the rider rather than the horse often wins the prize and grabs the glory. At rodeos, the horses are often not even mentioned by name to the spectators. Nor is a record kept of their sex or identity, although most of the riders certainly know just who their top equine competition is. One cattle event does give credit to the horse, and rightly so. That is cutting.

Cutting

Cutting, the fastest growing in participation and prize money and by far the best promoted of the cattle sports, requires horse and rider to ride into a small herd, select one cow, and demonstrate an ability to thwart the animal's attempt to return to the herd. The more determined the cow, the more points the horse is able to win. The sport simulates the practical ranch work of separating individual animals for special treatment or handling.

On the ranch, only the bottom line counts. If horse and rider keep the correct individual from returning to the herd, they succeed. In the arena, the pair has to show a little more style. In cutting competition, it's not just what you do but how you do it and how fast you do it.

More than any other equine sport, cutting is a horse's game. Yes, a human has to get the horse into the arena at the proper time, since even the most intelligent cutter is unlikely to have figured out the intricacies of the draw. The rider also has to help in selecting the calf or steer in order to pick one that will allow them to show off their skills to the judges. Occasionally, even this is handled by the horse.

Old-timers like to tell the story about the legendary cutting mare Marion's Girl, whose rider Buster Welch suffered an eye injury before a competition in San Francisco. He could barely see the herd when he went into the ring, so Marion's Girl picked her own cow—choosing a difficult, showy one—and worked it to perfection.

Most cutting horses aren't Marion's Girl and most riders like to pick out their own cows to work. But after that, winning is up to the horse. Riders are required to drop their reins, and if the judges spot a rider giving a rein signal to the horse, the team loses points.

The nature of the competition suits most athletic mares. In cutting, the horse is at the very least an equal participant in the entire process, and the typical independent-thinking mare will thrive in such an atmosphere.

Cutting horse trainer and breeder Kim Estes removes the bridle from his top cutting mare Dillon Spy for demonstrations. She amazes crowds with her ability to confound cows bareheaded. For competition, she wears a bridle, but when she needs direction, it isn't from anything as obvious as a pull on a rein or even a kick.

"You can make a mare like this run sideways just by laying the calf of your leg on her," Estes says. He points out that Dillon Spy, like most other good cutting horses, is short-haired, thin-skinned, and very sensitive to the touch. The extreme sensitivity that frustrates trainers of mares in some of the other equine sports is a tremendous advantage in cutting.

The nature of the competition suits her in another way, too. Estes doesn't believe that either anger or misplaced foal concentration is involved in his mare's love of her sport. "This mare's playing a game," he says. "She's addicted to cattle like some men are addicted to golf."

Dillon Spy may not have perfect conformation, but her most important physical qualities—a superb set of hindquarters and outstanding flexibility—are more than enough to make her well suited to the sport. "She folds and bends," Estes says. "I've had this mare wrap right around my leg to turn around. She's like a gymnast."

As much as any individual horse is typical, Dillon Spy has a

a

b

c

d

a,b,c,d Although Kim Estes usually works Dillon Spy in a bridle, this cutting demonstration without a bridle shows how much pure talent is involved. She fixes on the cow, challenges it and is relentless in keeping it from returning to the herd.

typical mare conformation, with the center of balance more to the rear than to the front, with substantial hindquarters and a comparatively small neck. It should come as no surprise that a typical mare conformation is nearly perfect for the sport of cutting. During much of the process of working a cow, the horse carries its weight on its hindquarters and rear legs, ready to wheel and move as the cow does. The horse with more weight to the rear will have an advantage, and the horse with too much weight up front suffers.

The fact that a mare may have a 5 or 6 percent disadvantage in cannon bone circumference compared to a male horse will be no problem in cutting, as it might be in the jumping sports or others where the front legs have to absorb sudden weight shock. Overall flexibility is important in cutting, and the generally lighter body weight of a mare helps in this area, too. Add to all this the fact that mares often have a healthy dose of cow sense, and it's easy to understand why so many mares compete at the highest levels of cutting.

Selecting a Cutting Mare

An active and functioning market exists for cutting horses. How well a horse does in competition generally speaks for the horse's ability, but buyers have to take one precaution beyond the normal health and soundness checks. Skilled cutting riders can give subtle rein cues to a horse that judges might not see or might choose to overlook. The same judges may not do the same for the next owner. Still, when you are looking to buy a horse already in competition, you can judge her ability prior to your purchase. Expect to spend a lot of money if she's any good.

"The mares get very expensive in a hurry," Estes says. A gelding can earn plenty in cutting competition, but a mare can earn just as much and provide something more: foals. In cutting breeding, that is significant. "Most great horses have great mothers," Estes says. "I believe that cutting ability seems to come more from the mare's side than from the stallion's side." A mare who has proven herself in cutting competition is invaluable in the breeding shed.

Other experts are equally convinced that cutting talent comes from the sire's side. Descendants of the great stallion Poco Bueno are still winning cutting events decades after the peak of his career. Of course, his most celebrated offspring was his daughter Poco Lena, twice World Champion and four times runnerup. Poco Lena was the first inductee into the National Cutting Horse Association Hall of Fame, and her blood is the most prized in the cutting horse world.

Most buyers will have to satisfy themselves with a cutting prospect, and that is obviously harder to pick. Conformation is important. Good hindquarters are necessary, and a Quarter Horse or other stock-type mare is likely to have them. The neck should not be too heavy, which it probably won't be in a mare who hasn't been receiving steroids. Short cannon bones are useful, as is a flexible back of medium length. A buyer can get an idea of flexibility and agility in a broken but not cutting-trained horse with simple figure eights, spins and other movements.

The horse should also be checked for quick reflexes. Does she react instantly to cues, or does she need time to think about them and get her legs together? A horse that seems to be extremely dependent on rein activity for her cues might be trainable for cutting, but she will probably require a lot of work and may never be capable of winning.

Cow sense is vital, and this quality is the most difficult to determine in an untrained horse. An unbroken mare must be observed. You may be able to notice a potential cutter's interest in smaller animals. If she watches a bounding dog without showing fear, or if she pays close attention to sheep or other livestock, she may be a likely candidate. One young mare who subsequently turned into a top cutter showed her inclinations early when, as a foal, she made a game out of harassing an unfortunate duck who tried to nest alongside a pond in the filly's paddock. The duck was skillfully kept apart from both eggs and pond whenever it made the mistake of waddling away from the nest.

Some trainers like to ride a broken prospect right into a herd of calves. If the horse pays close attention to them, shows an inclination to follow them or demonstrates an interest in getting right in among them, she may have some useful "cow." Unfortunately, some horses have an interest in cows but little interest in cutting. That is usually not discovered until the horse is well along in training.

Cow sense is valuable in the other cattle events, and a similar procedure could be tried with prospects. But unlike cutting, pure speed is just as important in these other cow events.

Steer Wrestling

Steer wrestling, or bull dogging, is a rodeo event in which horses tend to get limited credit. The fans may not realize how important the horse is to the rider's success, but the riders certainly do. A skilled bull-dogging horse is both cherished and profitable. A rider lucky enough to own one can make money off it himself and can also rent it to other riders for a percentage of their winnings.

Steer wrestling requires horse and rider to break out of a chute a heartbeat behind the steer, catch up with the streaking animal, then position themselves alongside. When the moment is right, the rider jumps off and wrestles the steer to the ground, and the horse gets itself out of the way. The horse needs cow sense, although perhaps not quite so much as in cutting. But it still has to be able to judge a steer's gait and pace, anticipate any evasive moves and be prepared to adjust its own position. A steer-wrestling horse has to understand steers.

It also has to be quick—extremely quick—out of the gate, able to get to full speed almost instantly and keep up the speed for just a few seconds. This means that good hindquarters and relatively light body weight will help the horse. In addition, a good bull-dogging horse shouldn't be too tall, since the rider doesn't want a long drop to the ground. The horse has to be able to make its own decisions, because the speed of the event prevents the rider from giving many cues. Again, it's no surprise that many cowboys choose mares for their steer-wrestling mounts. They are extremely well suited, mentally and physically, for the task. Some rodeo performers are reluctant to deal with heat cycles and prefer geldings, but others wouldn't change their light, quick mares for anything.

The most beloved of all steer-wrestling horses was Baby Doll, who became nationally known when she was featured in *Life* magazine in the late 1950s. The small bay mare won hundreds of events for dozens of riders, and her sudden death of colic in 1960 had tough cowboys throughout the West shedding tears for her.

Roping

Roping competitions are most familiar to rodeo fans, where the calf—and sometimes steer—roping event is often the climax of the entire rodeo. Western horse shows sometimes include calf roping, too, but show roping is judged differently. Style and manners count as much as quickness in show competition, while in rodeo roping, pure speed wins.

In the rodeo, horse and rider burst out of the starting gate after the calf is released. The horse gets the rider in good position to throw his rope, keeps going after the throw, then slides itself to a stop when it feels the rider leaving the saddle. It then remains in a position to keep the rope tied to the saddle taut (but not so tight that the roped calf struggles) while the cowboy ties the legs of the animal. Most of these actions are taken by the horse independently. It knows what to do and does it.

Mentally, the sport is suited to mares, many of whom like to work independently, and many of whom like to chase cattle. The physical requirements in terms of quick starts, agility and sliding stops suit mares, too. Many good roping horses are mares, but—unlike cutting and steer wrestling—male horses usually make up a much higher percentage of mounts in top competition.

One reason for this may be that weight in the front end helps a little in roping, and males are somewhat more likely to have extra weight in the neck and shoulders. After the roping horse slides to a stop, he leans back to maintain a taut rope. His body weight competes against that of the calf or steer, and extra strength in front of the saddle helps.

The pressure of the marketplace may be another reason why there are comparatively fewer mares in top-level calf roping than in the other cattle sports. Since calves are extremely quick, speed out of the gate is very important in calf roping. The best source of quick-getaway speed is the Quarter Horse racetrack, and many good roping horses come right off the track after their racing careers end. If they have the necessary speed to be good roping horses, they were probably pretty good racehorses too. A pretty good race mare is usually more valuable as a broodmare than as a roping horse, while a pretty good racing gelding—once he has finished racing—has to find another line of work.

But mares can and do excel in roping. In 1982 the four-year-old Sweet And Innocent became World Champion calf-roping horse. She also placed in reining and working cow horse events in that year's AQHA World Championship Show, earning herself the title of Superhorse for 1982. The versatile Sweet And Innocent carried three different riders in the five events she entered.

The Speed Sports

The Quarter Horse, the dominant breed in western competition, is a natural speedster. The breed was developed and nurtured to create an animal who can reach top speed in a minimum of strides and then maintain that speed for distances as short as a handful of yards and as long as a quarter mile. Most western sports showcase this quality of quick bursts of speed at some point during the event. Two sports in particular place an additional premium on it, and in both sports mares either play or are capable of playing an equal role with male horses.

Barrel Racing and Other Timed Events

Barrel racing, as well as pole bending, flag relays and other timed competitions, requires horse and rider to gallop through a course that includes turns and changes of direction. The fastest time wins. Form doesn't matter, nor does style—only the clock counts. In barrel racing, the most popular of the timed events, the competitors complete a cloverleaf pattern around three barrels placed 30 to 40 yards apart, the distance depending on the rules of the particular organization sponsoring the event. The event can be part of a rodeo, gymkhana, horse show or a competition devoted exclusively to barrel racing.

The sport was begun in the 1940s to provide a rodeo event for women, and although nowadays men compete, too, women still dominate. The lighter weight of female riders probably helps the horses as they circle the barrels as closely as possible, then burst into top speed to head to the next turn. Not only do women dominate, but lighter women seem to do best of all.

As for the sex of the horse, most barrel-racing riders and trainers have no strong preference. They want horses with the speed to gallop the straightaways, the agility to complete a close, accurate turn and the competitive nature to make a determined effort in the excitement and confusion of a show or rodeo. These qualities come in both sexes.

"I don't care whether it's a mare or gelding," says top East Coast competitor and barrel-racing coach Ginger Crotta. "When I'm looking for a good barrel prospect it first has to appeal to me. It has to be clean-legged and it has to have a nice underline to it. The bone structure has to be sturdy because it's going to have to take a lot of concussion, and it has to have a muscular rear end because a lot of work is done off the back end. But you have to have something streamlined, too—something built for speed. Mares are often a little more streamlined, and I have no qualms about competing on a mare."

In fact, Ginger competed for some time on a good mare she called Blue, winning numerous events around the country. Blue, she says,

Pole bending, like other timed events, is well suited to mares. This mare's tremendous hindquarters and comparatively light body weight allow her to fly on the straightaways, yet cut within inches of the poles.

was probably her quickest-ever learner, winning her first buckle less than a year after going into training. Blue also helped convince Ginger that estrus is not necessarily a problem for barrel-racing mares.

"It seemed like she was in heat every weekend when she competed, but it didn't really affect her performance at all. She might raise her tail sometimes, but it never bothered her running."

Barrel racing, like the other galloping sports, gives mares in heat less time to think about—and be distracted by—their hormonal urges. Ginger Crotta, like many other barrel riders and trainers, believes moody and grouchy horses come in both sexes, as do horses who are easy to get along with and consistent in their outlook on life.

Ginger acknowledges that an intelligent horse can get bored and soured by too much work in the invariable pattern of the barrel race. Alert mares are particularly good candidates for variation. But they still need work to keep in shape.

"My barrel horses are in lessons," Ginger says. "I rope off them, and I trail ride off them. But my horses seldom run the pattern when they're not competing. I'll do slow work, maybe walk, trot, lope them around the barrels. This way they think the competitive run is special." A horse who has done poorly on a competitive run might get some galloping around the barrels so Ginger can figure out what went wrong, but a trained barrel horse saves its run for the ring.

Although mares don't necessarily make better barrel racers than stallions or geldings, they certainly don't seem to be inferior. Nor are they inferior in the other—more lucrative—western speed sport.

Short Track Racing

Most sanctioned short track racing is conducted under the authority of the American Quarter Horse Association, but there is organized Appaloosa racing, as well as less common—and more informal—

Paint and Pinto racing, and even less common mule racing. The Quarter Horse events offer the biggest prize money, the largest crowds and the fastest times. At the highest levels of the sport, Quarter Horse racing has come to emulate Thoroughbred racing in everything but the distances. The appendix registration rule of the AQHA, which allows one Thoroughbred parent, has even created a situation where today's successful racing Quarter Horses are usually at least three-quarters Thoroughbred. But although Quarter Horse racing may look a great deal like Thoroughbred racing these days, there is one significant difference. In short racing, nobody is surprised when a mare is fastest of all.

Quarter Horse racing has failed to catch on with any degree of permanence outside the western United States. In spite of repeated efforts to establish and maintain a foothold east of the Mississippi, it remains identified with the West. Even though the first quarter-mile races took place in the eastern seaboard colonies in the seventeenth and eighteenth centuries, today's sport can be traced more directly to nineteenth-century match races down dusty streets in small western towns, mostly in Texas and Louisiana.

The names still remembered 150 years after these unrecorded races are almost all male. Among the great racehorses of the Texas towns were Steel Dust and Old Billy and Copperbottom, but we know about these and other horses of the mid-nineteenth century not so much for their racing exploits but because their names have come down in pedigrees. Some mares raced and won and produced important foals, but the sheer volume of offspring means that the great old-time stallions are the ones whose names we remember.

There are individual exceptions. Della Moore, foaled in Louisiana some time after 1905, was a brilliant short-course runner, probably the fastest horse in the country at her peak just before World War One. But Della Moore was an even more valuable broodmare, becoming the dam of Joe Reed, one of the three foundation sires of the Quarter Horse breed. That fact ensures that modern admirers of short-running mares remember at least one from the early days of the sport.

The AQHA was formed in 1940 and it provided the impetus

for organized, controlled and recorded short racing. When that happened, mares galloped right to the front. Around 1940 the stallion Clabber was the reigning short-race champion of the world. But his time at the top was brief.

On February 18, 1942, the modern sport saw its first great race, when the five-year-old sorrel mare Shue Fly challenged Clabber in the World Champion Quarter Horse race in Tucson, Arizona. Shue Fly tripped coming out of the gate and fell to her knees, but she made up the seven lengths she lost to catch and pass Clabber in the final strides of the 440-yard race. The huge crowd was stunned, as were later crowds in other places, as Shue Fly raced to win after win throughout the Southwest. She was the best, not just the best mare.

Clabber was never able to regain his World Champion title, and when Shue Fly finally relinquished it in 1945, it went to a mare named Queenie. She was in turn overtaken for championship honors by Miss Princess. Barbra B never quite made World Champion, but she made the world take notice when she easily beat the Johnny Longden–ridden Thoroughbred colt Fair Truckle in a match race at Hollywood Park in 1947. Barbra B earned the right of an entire breed to call itself "the world's fastest horse."

Eight of the first ten recognized World Champions of Quarter Horse racing were mares. In 1950, a stallion with the unlikely name of Blob Jr. regained some respect for male Quarter Horses when he became champion, but his reign was short. Three mares in a row followed him at the top of the Quarter Horse heap.

After the mid-1950s, mares, stallions, fillies, colts and geldings set records and earned honors in nearly equal proportions. Anybody who could remember the 1940s would never have dreamed of suggesting that short-running mares were anything less than equal to male runners. Until enough years dimmed the memory, most people involved in Quarter Horse racing might have even said that mares were probably a little faster.

By the 1970s, colts and stallions had come to the forefront. Flashy, highly publicized horses like Jet Deck, Easy Jet, Dash For Cash and Special Effort got most of the attention. They were stallions, and therefore they were worth a fortune in money and publicity. Quarter racing fans began to think that males must be a little faster than mares after all. That is probably the prevailing attitude today, but people sometimes have to overlook reality to hold on to it.

Here are some random examples that clearly refute the "male must be faster" idea. In 1969, as the age of the stallion was about to begin, the AQHA recognized world records at seven distances, ranging from 220 to 440 yards. Five of the seven records were held by mares.

Move ahead twenty years. In August and September of 1989, Ruidoso Downs, the crown jewel of American short tracks, held the racing season's three premier events for Quarter Horses. One race each for two-year-olds, three-year-olds and older horses offered a total of nearly $3 million in purse money. The two-year-old filly Strawberry Silk won the All-American Futurity, the three-year-old filly See Me Do It won the All-American Derby, and the four-year-old mare Dash For Speed won the All-American Gold Cup. It was a two-week display of intergenerational dominance.

Such a display of female superiority doesn't happen every year; still, fillies and mares regularly win major open events. They carry equal weights and qualify for the big-money finals on a fifty-fifty basis. In 1989, for example, fifteen of the twenty-nine qualifiers for the three Ruidoso events were female. It's not a subject for comment when a filly or mare wins a big race, because it happens far too often.

This has remained true into the 1990s in spite of the development during the seventies and eighties of a full schedule of distaff races, in which mares have to compete only against their own sex. There are plenty of races to enter and plenty of money to win in events that draw entries from a smaller pool of horses. Even so, fillies and mares still venture beyond their own division and still win.

Furthermore, many well-bred fillies get less chance to compete than male horses (as in Thoroughbred racing, a male needs a good race record to make a stud prospect while a female can get by with good bloodlines) and you reach a nearly inescapable conclusion. The Greeks may have been right after all. Mares, on average, may just be a little faster than male horses—at least over short distances. There may be identifiable physical and mental reasons for this.

A Mind for Racing

Quarter-mile racing requires the physical ability to get up to high speed quickly, but it also requires the mental ability to get the legs and body moving in a split second. A good racing Quarter Horse must be alert, because a blown start is almost impossible to overcome. The natural alertness of mares dovetails well with this requirement. A proper break from the gate requires a horse to be so ready that a good-starting horse is often a nervous or edgy horse. Those are two adjectives often applied to racing mares.

The distractions of estrus might compromise the chances of a mare in a controlled performance event, but hormones have less chance to affect a sprint at top speed. An alert, aware filly is a fine prospect for success in the mental aspects of short racing.

Conformation for Racing

Every trainer, breeder and owner of Quarter Horses will tell you that good ones come in all shapes and sizes, and that crooked legs, bad necks and weak backs can and do show up in the winner's circle. But they will tell you just as quickly that they wouldn't pick a horse with these flaws, given a choice. Tastes in conformation vary slightly, but most Quarter racing people want the same things: a long, deep hip for power and quick getaway, a short back but a long underline for greater stride length, a deep, sloping shoulder for reach and a streamlined neck for speed.

Heavy-necked horses simply don't run as fast as others, all else being equal. Heavy body weight in general seems to slow down a horse, particularly at shorter distances where quick getaway plays a big role. In addition, since weight-carrying ability generally doesn't come into play until a horse faces a longer distance, heavier horses lose that advantage, too. For Quarter Horse racing, most experts want a horse under 16 hands—even under 15 is often acceptable—and in the 1,000-pound range.

A successful Quarter Horse should have enough strong, flat bone to withstand concussion, though. Review the statistics that tell us that a male has 10 percent more body weight but only 4 to 6 percent greater bone than a similar female, and it becomes easier to understand why female racing Quarter Horses have been so successful. All in all, a correct mare of typical female conformation fits the description of the ideal racing Quarter Horse.

Judged Events

When human judgment rather than measurable performance counts, typical mare conformation and mare behavior sometimes don't work out quite so well. A mare's work in precision events can be affected by estrus, and how that affects her score depends on what she does and what the judge thinks about it. Her overall appearance and style may be graded up or down, depending on whether the judge (or the breed) places a premium on relative delicacy or on a more masculine image.

Reining

Thousands of people compete with mares in reining events, and many of them have great success. They find mares to be good learners who master the intricate patterns of reining competition rapidly and thoroughly. Their rear-oriented center of gravity helps in the sliding stop, the pivot and other requirements of the sport. But reining requires much of the same precise control that dressage does. Whether it's because mares may be a little less enthusiastic about following specific orders, or whether it's a result of human prejudice that comes into judging decisions and owner choice, mares are not quite as heavily used as stallions and geldings in top reining competition. The percentage of mares is not nearly as small as it is in dressage, but males do seem to hold the upper hand.

This does not mean that a person hoping to compete in reining should avoid mares. Many trainers are convinced mares learn more quickly, retain what they've learned longer and often enjoy the competitive nature of shows more than male horses do. Among recent outstanding reining mares is Eye Docs Mistie, who far out-pointed all other AQHA reining horses in 1986, and Diamonds Sparkle, whose reining performance in the 1979 Superhorse competition made her the second straight winner of that event. But most reining champions of the past several years have been males.

If you do rein with a mare, you can't do anything about judges' preferences, but you can make it a point to enjoy the sense of partnership with your horse. It's a sensation that can feel as good as winning.

Trail and Western Pleasure Classes

The demands on horses in these show classes are somewhat less precise than those in reining, but a distracted horse will still lose points, and a judge who thinks a masculine look equates with good style may take away even more points from a mare. But some judges like the streamlined look, and a mare can learn to resist her hormonal urges in the ring. So a mare can be a useful mount in the subjectively judged western classes, where a horse's appearance, manners, and "suitability" play a part in its success.

Still, many competitors in these events are likely to claim that they would choose a gelding over a mare, all else being equal. They wouldn't turn down a magnificently conformed, perfectly trained mare, but if a mare and a gelding were equal in conformation and talent, most would lean toward the gelding. The judges, they think, prefer male appearance and manners.

But this is not true in most western events, certainly the ones where performance alone counts. In fact, anyone who likes a good western-trained horse, whether for competition or casual riding, will probably find that companionship, partnership and sheer physical ability will outweigh any real or presumed problems that mares might cause. I have a barrel-trained Quarter Horse mare myself, and Annie's occasional springtime tail lifting is a small price to pay for her intelligence, agility and friendship.

8

The Pleasure Mare

IN TERMS OF SIMPLE NUMBERS MORE ATHLETIC HORSES NEVER COM-
pete for prize money or ribbons than do. Their dollar value may
be less, but their emotional worth is greater. They simply perform
for a different audience. These are the horses who provide sport
and companionship for their owners—the pleasure horses on whom
we lavish time, money and love. Mares figure prominently in each
of the categories of pleasure horse, largely because their personalities so often suit the work.

A mare whose reluctance to be turned into a push-button machine
might make her a difficult dressage horse yet she can be ideally
suited to field hunting. A mare whose seasonal lapses of concentration might ruin a jumping round will do no harm and might even
provide extra entertainment on a casual trail ride. In activities where
a rider needs a companion and partner rather than a slave, a mare
will excel.

Field Hunters

Mares have long been a significant presence in the hunting field. They remain so, even though hunting itself becomes less of a presence each year. Between subdivisions and construction and anti-blood sport movements, fewer and fewer packs lead fields of jumpers across meadows, streams and fences. A number of organized hunts remain, primarily in the central and southeastern United States, and thousands of horses are still active in hunting.

There are probably even more horses involved in drag hunts, where no live quarry is chased, as well as organized hunter paces, where riders can experience the thrill of the hunt without the expense of the hounds and the problems of obtaining rights to cross private property without advance notice. Hunter paces may be a little less thrilling than the traditional hunt, since the rider goes into action knowing in advance a great deal about the route and the obstacles. But they do provide much of the atmosphere of the hunt, and they do require a horse who is suitable to the hunting field. The better the horse might be at following the hounds, the better he or she will be in a more informal hunt situation.

Actually, almost any horse can hunt. Even the traditional hound pack is likely to be followed by a motley assortment of animals, including heavyweight crossbreds, fast and handsome Thoroughbreds and a few fat ponies carrying children bringing up the rear. But only certain horses can hunt well, and the horse who fits the category of "good hunter" is as likely to be female as male.

Most good field hunters carry a hefty dose of Thoroughbred blood and many are registered Thoroughbreds. Even the heavy hunters are often half-bred Thoroughbred, with the other half being draft or warmblood. Registered warmbloods show up in the hunting field, too, but a warmblood owner who thinks his horse isn't largely Thoroughbred should look at its pedigree through half a dozen generations. The Thoroughbred blood is necessity, not fashion.

Of all breeds, the Thoroughbred seems to best combine the speed required to follow fast hounds, sufficient stamina at the trot and canter to allow the rider to hunt three or more hours at a stretch

Hunters need sturdy conformation. Marilyn is a show hunter pony, but her good shoulder, strong hindquarters, and substantial bone could take her comfortably into the field.

and scope enough to handle any tall or wide obstacles that appear in the field. When a true heavyweight hunter is needed to carry a 200-pound rider, a prospective buyer may seek out a horse with Thoroughbred blood combined with that of a breed that offers a little more cannon bone and a larger skeletal frame. But a Thoroughbred—even a female one—whose sire and dam were selected specifically for substance and bone will be capable of handling the weight of almost any rider.

The Thoroughbred is a breed—like the Quarter Horse—that seems to produce good mares, and this may be a key to understanding why female field hunters are so widely used. The "ideal" Thoroughbred structure—good hindquarters, adequate but not heavy neck and shoulder, long body but not necessarily long back—is a structure that mares are inclined toward anyway. The presumed Thoroughbred temperament—alert, competitive, maybe a little nervous—is something more likely to be seen in a mare than a gelding of any breed. Mares do extremely well in sports where Thoroughbred blood predominates, and field hunting is no exception.

Conformation

Show ring hunters need a particular, acceptable conformation, even those who appear in working hunter classes where conformation is not supposed to count except in general terms of suitability. It does count, and everybody knows it. What's wanted in the show ring may actually vary from year to year. Hunter judging is highly subjective, and fashions in hunter conformation change. But physical appearance—not just grooming and turnout—matters a great deal in hunter classes of all kinds. The judges are looking for an idealized version of a field hunter, with the exception that pony hunters may—obviously—be smaller than most people would like to take into the field.

Field hunters may be any size and shape that allows them to gallop hard and jump obstacles of modest height. They don't even have to be overtly suitable. They can be ugly or misshapen and still perform admirably. But the fact remains that certain conformation characteristics appear in most of the best field hunters. These characteristics can easily be found in mares, and, in fact, some occur more often in mares.

The ideal hunter will have some height, preferably 16 hands or more, since the 4-foot fence pops up occasionally in the field. While mares are a little shorter than male horses of similar breeding, the difference is only about half an inch in the 16.2-hand horse. The difference is not enough to make a mare less able to jump a hunt course simply because of her sex.

The ideal hunter will have strong hindquarters, but it will have a long, slender neck. The nature of jumping in the field is different from that in open jumper competition, where the heavy male neck helps pull the body over the enormously tall jumps that have become so common in the ring. The field hunter is expected to jump wide and low, and weight in front is relatively less useful. Mares, compared to stallions and geldings, carry a greater percentage of their weight behind.

The ideal hunter will be a bit lighter in the body than another athletic horse of similar size. Some healthy field hunters are so thin that a conformation hunter judge in a show ring would call the vet before allowing them to compete. A horse can't easily carry great body weight over miles of countryside—running, jumping and constantly moving forward for as long as five hours without a break. Mares, since they average as much as 10 percent less body weight than related male horses, have a built-in advantage in this category.

The ideal hunter has extremely healthy and strong feet, neither too small nor too large for its height and weight. In fact, some experienced hunt riders insist that a well-made set of hoofs is the single most important characteristic of the good field hunter. The hoofs, particularly the front ones, take tremendous abuse during a hunt. They may pound on pavement or pick their way among pebbles at all four gaits. The front hoofs will certainly take a pounding as the horse jumps obstacles. Sex alone does not make a mare's feet more or less healthy than a male horse's, but her relatively lighter body weight seems to help protect her from some hoof conditions caused by stress, such as navicular disease.

Male hunters do have an advantage in one category. Some kinds of field hunting are performed most easily by a horse with substantial bone, particularly a short, dense cannon bone. A hunt over open country with firm going and lots of high jumps is best handled by a horse with heavy bone. This is somewhat more likely to be found in male horses, who have as much as a 6 percent advantage in cannon bone circumference in the Thoroughbred and near-Thoroughbred breeds. Wooded country with ditches to cross and modest barriers to jump presents no such requirements.

Mares with good cannon bone can be found, certainly. Remember this, too: If a mare (or male, for that matter) is light in bone, she doesn't have to jump every obstacle that presents itself during the hunt. Most can be gone around. No rider is ever thought less of for protecting his horse. It's far worse to leave the hunt early with a lame horse than to go around a jump.

Mental Requirements

Not every horse is psychologically suited to hunting. Some have behavioral tendencies that make them unpleasant or even dangerous in the field. Neither male nor female horses are more likely to have personality characteristics that make them bad hunters. Poor handling or training, rather than gender, causes most vices, although some tendencies may be inherited.

The one thing a successful field hunter *cannot* be is spooky. It should never bolt, shy at an unexpected sight or sound, or stop without warning. The one thing it *must* be is bold. A field hunter is asked to cross territory and negotiate barriers it probably has never seen before.

Some mares are spooky or timid, and they should not be used in the hunting field unless you are desperate for a mount. Some geldings are also spooky or timid, and they, too, should stay out of the field. Other mares (and geldings) are bombproof and bold, but these admirable characteristics are not a result of their sex.

Many riders are convinced that mares are more nervous than geldings and thus more likely to be untrustworthy in the field.

Whether there is any truth in this depends on your definition of "nervous." If you equate "nervous" with "spooky," then it's not true. Mares are not more nervous than geldings, unless early treatment has given them the idea that shying and bouncing around is acceptable behavior when they spot something new and frightening.

If you equate "nervous" with "alert" or "on edge," then it may be true. Empirical evidence exists to suggest that entire horses—both mares and stallions—are more alert and observant then geldings. It would require lots of observation of lots of horses to prove it, but the sexual nature of horses and the circumstances of their lives in the wild apparently make unaltered horses somewhat more aware of changes in their environment and more concerned about threats than geldings.

There's nothing wrong with this in the hunting field. Properly channeled, alertness can contribute greatly to the mental makeup of a good field hunter. In the hands of a poor rider, however, alertness and excitement can be a problem, creating a horse who hunts her own line, makes her own decisions about what to jump and what is best avoided and refuses to submit to the wishes of the rider.

Mares usually have no problem with another necessary mental characteristic for successful hunting. Hunters have to be willing to go in company, whether alongside, in front of or behind other horses. In the wild, mares are happiest with plenty of close company. They lead, trail and walk alongside other mares on a regular basis, although they choose their own order when free of riders. Even thoroughly domesticated mares spend plenty of time in company. Mares are usually turned out in groups, stallions never and geldings somewhere in between.

Mares may be a little more likely to kick than other horses, and kickers are dreaded in the hunting field. They are relegated to the back of the pack, their tails marked with telltale red ribbons. But the fact that the mare's natural defense is the kick does not mean that a mare with a rider aboard is necessarily going to be a kicker. Each is an individual, and each should be tested with rides in company before she's trucked to the field.

In fact, work in company—both on the flat and over fences—

should be used as part of the test for the mental characteristics necessary for good hunting long before the mare is ever actually tried with a hunt. Try her over fences, at the trot, and at the canter in front of, behind and alongside other horses, male and female. Then canter her past crumpled-up papers, introduce her to dogs, observe her when birds dart into view. Present her with as many different potential barriers as you can find. A mare who jumps 4-foot rail fences with enthusiasm may unexpectedly refuse a much smaller solid bank. She may think that monsters lurk at the bottom of a 3-inch-deep stream.

She should be road safe, too. A huntsman will try to keep the pack away from roads, but dogs following a scent don't always listen, and they never carry maps. If a mare has problems with any of these situations, don't consider her to be automatically disqualified from hunting. Discovering them in advance will allow you to accustom her to them and to be aware of potential difficulties when you are in the field.

Hunting mares don't have one problem that mares in other sports often do. Hunts take place when fields are not planted, from mid-autumn until late winter. In the southern United States, the hunting season usually ends no later than mid-February. Further north, it will probably be over by mid-March. This means that hunting mares almost never have to worry about estrus, and their owners don't have to worry about mounts whose minds are occupied by something other than their work.

The Riding Mare

The vast majority of horse owners do not have access to the hunting field, ambition to hunt or a horse capable of handling a five-hour jaunt over dozens of obstacles. They may do a little easy jumping with their horses, or teach them some elementary dressage, or try some of the moves of the reining or barrel horse. But what they really want is a horse to ride, mostly at the walk and trot, over trails and in the ring. They need a companion who is willing and athletic enough to meet the demands of the work.

There are millions of horses like this in North America, and millions more in the rest of the world. Nobody has any real statistics, but there are probably more geldings than mares working as riding horses.

The assumption that mares are difficult may be part of the reason for this. As we've seen, mares don't have to be more difficult than geldings, but inexperienced horse owners—and even some experienced ones—may have heard such horror stories about estrus that they want to avoid it and the mares likely to suffer it at all costs. In reality, mares are not in heat very often, and even when they are it rarely has much effect on casual riding use.

My own Quarter Horse mare Annie goes through long, intense heat periods in the spring. It means more work for me, but it doesn't mean she is any less useful. Normally, she goes forward with just the slightest pressure on her sides, and makes a turn with the most delicate touch of rein. When she's in heat and has stopped to lift her tail to a particularly attractive gelding in a nearby field, she requires more than gentle pressure. But she does go forward and she does turn. Her personality, even in heat, makes up for any extra effort that becomes necessary when her hormones get the better of her.

A mare in heat should be subject to the same discipline as a horse not in heat, within reason. She shouldn't be punished for her interest in breeding, but neither should she be allowed to stop and display herself for more than the second or two it takes you to discover that she is doing it. She is capable of learning that she must keep her interest to herself when she is under saddle.

People who do use mares for casual riding will find they enjoy their mares more if they pay special attention to their particular needs. Riding horses are often allowed to slip into unvarying routine. To a point, that's good, since horses feel secure and comfortable with routine. They like to be fed at the same time, to be turned out at the same time, to have their stalls cleaned at the same time. But their riding time should be varied, to keep up their level of interest and as well as your own. This appears to be particularly important with unaltered horses, whose extra alertness is best utilized by teaching new skills and perfecting old ones.

Vary your mare's routine as much as possible. Change your trail

Willingness to follow makes mares good candidates for electric hotwalkers.

route so she has something different to look at, even if this involves riding around so you start with the section you usually finish on. Add new skills, even simple ones—perhaps you can develop a pivot out of her existing ability to stop and back. Trot her in a serpentine around the ring, rather than a plain circle, and then add a figure eight. You will find that you both will enjoy your daily ride more. All animals need stimulation in their lives, humans and horses included. It's possible to get stimulation and still have the relaxing experience that you want from horse ownership.

Almost all horses prefer going out in the company of other horses, but mares may enjoy it even more than geldings. Most will happily join a string, following along nose to tail. The occasional kicker must be identified and kept to the rear of the string.

If one mare seems particularly determined to lead the string, it might be wise to allow her to do so. The alpha mare is an inevitable part of natural equine life. She leads and the rest of the horses follow. Alpha-hood is sometimes determined by fighting, but often the horses in a group seem to know who's boss without any visible evidence of how the election was held. It doesn't always show up in ridden horses, but the domestication has done nothing to snuff out this basic and essential characteristic of horses.

If you find yourself in a string that has appointed itself an alpha mare, let her go first. You'll have a happier trail ride with more enthusiastic equine partners. Just make sure that the rider aboard Miss Alpha knows the route you plan to take.

Racehorse and other high-volume trainers find that the willingness of fillies to follow other horses makes them especially suitable for cooling out on the electric hotwalker. Even a highly nervous filly usually settles right into the endless following that the hotwalker provides.

The School Mare

Lesson horses for beginners have to be absolutely trustworthy, which mares and geldings are equally capable of being. But the economics of riding schools being what they are, lesson horses have to be able to work day after day, with no exceptions for estrus. A beginning rider may not be able to get any work out of a mare whose hormones are calling. In addition, the average mare is probably more sensitive to abuse than the average gelding, and she may not make quite as satisfactory a mount for a heavy-handed beginner as the gelding.

At the intermediate level, most mares become more appropriate as lesson horses. Riders can coax movement out of them regardless of the season, and mares can provide plenty of action. In fact, they may be preferable for intermediate students, since part of the post-beginner schedule should be learning how to deal with horses' physical and mental quirks and with individual equine personalities.

At the highest level of rider training, probably fewer mares than geldings are in use. It's still a question of economics. For example, the ideal school horse for top-level dressage training is a retired top-level horse, one who can do all the moves although perhaps not with the animation he used to manage. A mare who fits that category is likely to be retired to the breeding farm because her owner hopes she can produce foals with her own quality.

None of this means that mares can't make good school horses. I first learned to ride aboard a draft-cross mare named Russet, who would do what she was supposed to regardless of what you accidentally told her to do. I learned to jump aboard an enthusiastic Paint named Marble, who never saw a jump she wanted to refuse. I learned saddle seat equitation aboard a Morgan named Betsy, who knew what to do but wouldn't do it unless you got the aids exactly right. They were all school horses, all outnumbered by their gelding friends and all wonderful teachers.

A Mare Around the Barn

Mares need the same basic housing facilities as other horses, including shelter, free access to water and as much turnout as they can reasonably receive. But you will have a happier mare if you keep her natural characteristics in mind as you plan her stabling and turnout.

Stalls

A mare, like a stallion or gelding, will appreciate a stall big enough for her to turn around comfortably, and to lie down without banging herself against the sides, and clean enough so her feet stay dry. She will also appreciate a chance to see her barn mates, possibly even more than male horses do. In the wild, mares are inclined to develop extremely complex social relationships, which depend on contact with other mares.

Domestic mares also try to develop these relationships, which they will do with geldings if other mares are not available. They like to see their companions, and stalls with an open front that allow them to stick their head into the shed row and maintain visual contact with their companions make them comfortable and secure. A mare who spends most of the day turned out with other horses will not need this contact as much as one who spends most of her day in the barn.

The inclination of some mares to establish close friendships can have an occasional negative effect. First, there's the problem that develops when a friend dies or is transferred to another farm. The separation anxiety can be worse than weaning. Then there's the occasional mare who gets so attached to her best friend that the friendship negatively impacts on her performance.

Jumper trainer Thom Pollard tells of a top jumper mare who had to be stabled next to a rotating cast of equine characters. Otherwise, she would become quickly attached to one and would refuse to be vanned to competitions unless her friend came, too. But on the whole, most mares thrive when they are allowed to maintain contact with other horses. That's what nature tells them to do, and they are happiest when when they follow nature's rules.

A stall front with a dutch door or a stall guard also allows a mare more contact with people who walk down the shed row. Mares seem to thrive on vocal and physical contact with their people, they like to be talked to and patted, and they will get more of that if their heads can be out. You do have to watch out for nippers, although mares are a little less likely to nip at passing people

Mixed turnout usually works best in winter, when estrus doesn't cause jealousy and possessiveness.

than male horses. Of course, if a mare gets tasty treats on a regular basis, she is more likely to become a nipper when a treat isn't available.

Turnout

Horse people disagree about whether it's safe or wise to turn out mixed groups of mares and geldings. Some people have done it and suffered badly (or rather, the horses have suffered) while others report no problems. The potential difficulties seem to occur primarily during spring and summer, when mares are in and out of heat. Problems are much more rare in the winter. Unfortunately, the problems are hard to predict. Mares in heat vary in their reaction to geldings, and geldings vary in their response.

Some mares are only marginally less interested in geldings than they are in stallions during estrus. They will show to them, follow them around, push into them and act like pests. Geldings may respond with interest, sometimes even trying to mount. Or they may react with disgust, biting and kicking at the mare.

Other mares in estrus have no interest in geldings, but the geldings are plenty interested in them. This may cause another kind of fight. Sometimes two geldings will be interested in the same mare and will fight each other, only to have the winner, after the battle, discover an uninterested mare. Or he may find an interested one. Often, neither group is interested in the other even during the spring, and their owners have no problems.

The safest course would be to turn out mares and geldings in separate groups, if you have individual paddocks or corrals. If you have just one, watch closely when one of the mares is in heat until you're sure nobody is going to do physical damage to anybody else.

Even if you do have room for same-sex turnout, you're not home free. Mares may be rough with each other as they establish their order of dominance. They are unlikely to try to injure each other as stallions might, but there will certainly be some kicking and even nipping as the mares assert the authority they would like to have.

Mares often try to avoid landing kicks, but the occasional one likes to make contact. Watch these aggressive mares closely, particularly when they are shod behind.

Some people try to avoid the rough stuff altogether and turn out horses individually, but in reality any mare would rather be out for two hours in the company of another mare who dominates her than be out for one hour by herself. Mare dominance activity is usually over within a day or two of the mares' first being turned out together. Once the relationship is worked out, you rarely have to worry about renewed aggression until a new mare arrives.

9

Mare Health

SINCE FEMALE AND MALE HORSES ARE PHYSICALLY MORE SIMILAR THAN they are different, most of their health care needs are the same. With few exceptions, they require the same worming, vaccinations, hoof care and other routine health maintenance procedures.

Both sexes need regular dental care, including floating, smoothing and removal of wolf teeth. Although some male horses need dental work to keep their tushes under control, the dental needs of both sexes are the same.

Consult your vet or local cooperative extension agent for health recommendations, including those vaccinations particularly important in your area. If you worm and vaccinate your own horses, the only special care you need to take with a mare is dosage. Your mare may be so much lighter than the same-height gelding in the next stall that she needs a significantly lower dosage of a wormer or vaccine. The instructions on the package will tell you the correct dosage.

If you expect to breed your mare within the next year, her vaccination and worming schedules may be slightly different than those of other horses. See Chapter 10 for advice on that, but your vet should be your final authority on her care while she's in foal.

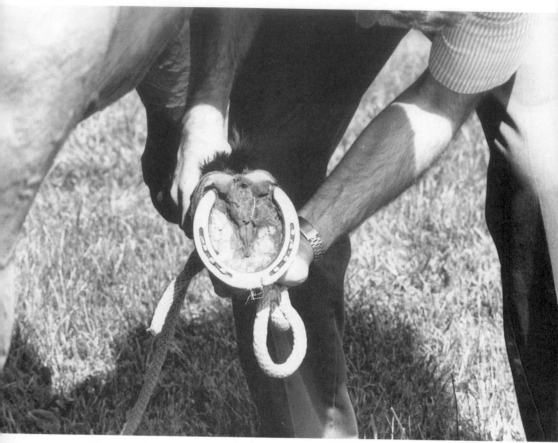

Mares are less subject to stress-related hoof disease, including navicular disease, probably because of their lighter average body weight.

Orthopedic Health

The structural differences between male and female horses don't seem to impact on a mare's health in any negative way. Studies of breakdowns at racetracks show no significantly greater incidence of skeletal or soft tissue injuries in mares, even though they have smaller, less dense cannon bones than related male horses. In fact, research indicates that skeletal injuries—as well as navicular disease and other foot problems—are more common in heavier horses. This suggests that mares might have a modest advantage over similar male horses in terms of orthopedic health.

Mares do break down, and they do suffer from navicular disease and virtually every other lameness problem known to man and horse. But they don't seem to suffer any worse than male horses in spite of their relatively lighter frames. All horses benefit from care in training and use, as well as from the owner's knowledge of the causes and treatment of lameness.

One problem, however, strikes mares more often than stallions or geldings. While it's not strictly orthopedic, azoturia (Monday morning disease) has the same effect by causing lameness and damaging the horse's ability to perform.

Azoturia

Horse people have been dealing with azoturia for centuries—ever since we began taking horses out of grazing pastures and housing them in stalls furnished with grain buckets. The condition used to be called Monday morning disease because of its characteristic appearance on the first working day of the week. Horses, like people, often got Sunday off, and only the most miserly owners would cut back on the animal's feed on the day of rest. On Monday morning an affected horse could be lured out of its stall only with the strongest urging. Pain, stiffness, inability to work and even permanent muscle injury could follow. In the most severe cases, the horse might die. The condition was never common, but it occurred often enough in valuable working horses to prompt considerable research into causes and treatments.

Azoturia, now called "tying-up" or "cording-up," still exists. We know more about it today, although we don't know everything. We don't know why mares in general—and fillies in particular—seem to be struck more often. We don't even know exactly what causes it, although we do know that the old-time horsemen were right. It most often strikes a horse who has been given rest and whose feed remains unchanged in spite of the reduction in workload. Athletic horses are the most likely victims, because they are most likely to be fed high-energy basic rations and to be given nutritional supplements to provide extra calories.

Azoturia is one of several so-called myopathies that affect horses. All these conditions involve the malfunction of muscle tissue, and they are caused by nutritional deficiencies, overwork, circulation problems, accident or unknown reasons. Azoturia is the most common myopathy and the one that affects mares more often than male horses.

Treatment consists mostly of careful management of the patient, and that must begin with the very first signs of the problem. The first symptoms are usually stiffness and rapid pulse, followed by increasing rigidity of the muscles, usually in the loins and back. Other symptoms include sweating, trembling, nervousness and hindquarter weakness or paralysis. A horse suffering from any myopathy should never be asked to continue its work. Even a walk back to the stall can lead to permanent muscle damage or death in a severe case of azoturia.

Horses who remain standing through the critical first day usually recover. Those who go down can also recover if they are kept quiet and don't stay down much longer than twenty-four hours. A vet will assure quiet by sedatives and tranquilizers if necessary. He or she will also run a blood test to check for elevated enzymes that indicate damage to muscle tissue and will check urine to see if there has been kidney damage.

Some vets have experimented with selenium and vitamin E injections to treat affected horses, and these nutritional treatments have had some success. There is no clear evidence that deficiencies of selenium or vitamin E lead to azoturia, but they are factors in other equine myopathies. So it was natural that they be tried in the treatment of azoturia, and they do seem to work in many cases. But researchers aren't quite ready yet to recommend supplementing the normal equine diet with these nutrients to help prevent the disease.

Obviously, it's far better to prevent azoturia than to try to treat it. The traditional method favored by old-time horsemen was to feed a wet bran mash the night before a day off. This may well be a good idea, but it's still necessary to cut back grain during the rest time, since there is an obvious correlation between excess energy level in feed and the appearance of azoturia in horses coming off a day or two of rest. Certainly, not all horses who are overfed while at rest develop the disease, but most who do have been fed too many calories. It does very occasionally occur in horses at grass, just to confuse the situation.

Nobody knows why mares tend to tie-up more often than stallions or geldings. It may be that many athletic mares are regularly given a greater volume of high-energy feed than they need. A 16.2 warmblood stallion may weigh 150 to 200 pounds more than a 16.2 warmblood mare. If the two are training and competing in the same sport, or doing equal pleasure work, the owner might be inclined to feed them the same amount of grain or pelleted feed. But greater weight in general requires more energy from feed just for maintenance, and greater weight in the form of muscle tissue requires even more energy, regardless of activity level.

If you own an athletic mare, consider keeping the total digestible energy content of her diet toward the low end of the recommended range for her size and activity, unless her condition or performance dictates otherwise. Also remember to plan the content of her diet according to her weight rather than her height, because she is likely to be lighter than a male horse of the same breed and height.

As for experimenting with selenium and vitamin E supplements, the evidence is not yet in as to whether they might help prevent tying-up. The wisest course is to make sure your mare gets enough (1.1 milligrams of selenium and 843 International Units of E a day for a working 1,000-pound horse) but to be wary of going over that level, since potential toxicity exists in large-scale supplementation. The National Research Council's *Nutrient Requirements of the Horse* has the latest information on what is known about nutritional needs of horses. See Recommended Reading for information on how to obtain it.

Some researchers think that hormones play a role in myopathies, including azoturia. No link has been established between female hormones and the condition, but it's possible that they are a triggering factor. Other hormones have been linked to other, much less common, myopathies, including those that appear in horses suffering from a deficiency of thyroid hormones. That deficiency is called hypothyroidism, and it, too, appears to be more common in female than male horses.

Hypothyroidism

Years ago, thyroid disorder was considered rare if not practically unknown in horses. More recently, Kentucky veterinarians searching for the cause of chronic infertility in otherwise healthy mares began doing blood tests on overweight, infertile animals. They discovered, to their surprise, that as many as 10 percent of the mares at the end of performance careers and headed to the breeding shed showed marked deficiency of thyroxine, the primary product of the thyroid gland. In addition to being infertile and overweight, many of the affected mares suffered stiffness and lethargy as well as an inability to shed in spring.

Researchers speculate that the stress of performance careers leads to the hypothyroidism in some young mares, yet blood tests also reveal the condition in mares who have been retired from competition for many years. As research continues, we may discover that male horses are equally affected by hypothyroidism, but most patients today are mares whose disease was brought to light by their infertility.

Hypothyroidism may be responsible for some otherwise unexplainable poor performance in athletic mares, since such a significant percentage of the recently retired mares tested on the Kentucky breeding farms turned up deficient. Tests for the condition will certainly become more common in performance animals as time goes by.

Hypothyroidism is easily treatable, and many labs can do the necessary blood work to discover a deficiency of T-3 and T-4, the two main thyroid hormones. The test costs less than fifty dollars, and the price will probably go down as testing becomes more widespread.

If a test turns up a shortage of a thyroid hormone, the mare will be treated with an oral powder supplement. The treatment can be permanent, with no detrimental effect on her health, or it can be stopped once her condition stabilizes. The supplement is added to feed and is readily swallowed by the mare. Thyroid treatments are becoming widely used at racetracks, particularly among hardworked Standardbreds who may start thirty or more times a year.

Thyroid supplementation must be done on the advice of a veterinarian, because excess amounts can cause as many problems as a deficiency. In addition to behavioral effects, too much supplementation may contribute to bone problems.

Uterine Infections

Uterine infection is much more common in mares who have foaled at some point in their lives, although it does appear regularly in mares who have been bred but turn up barren. It also appears occasionally in maiden mares. Some infections are strictly venereal in nature, so mares who have never been bred are not affected. Other infections are caused by common pathogens that can infect any mare, maiden or not, provided they have access to her uterus.

Some owners and vets are inclined to worry about infection only in mares intended for breeding, since an infected uterus can either prevent conception or limit the ability of a mare to carry her foal to term. But a badly infected performance or pleasure mare must

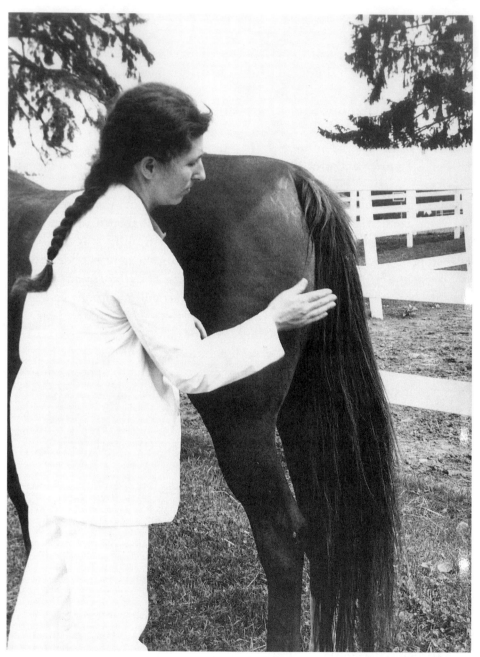

An examination for uterine infection should be done on all mares intended for breeding, and it's occasionally necessary for nonbreeding performance mares.

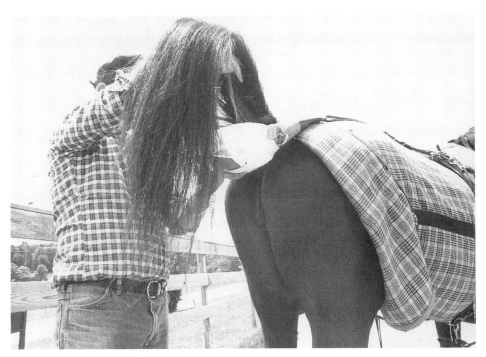

Tail sets and other equipment that comes in contact with the anal and genital regions of mares should be carefully placed and kept clean to avoid uterine infection.

It is a good idea for owners occasionally to check their mare's udder for the heat and inflammation of mastitis, even a mare that has not foaled.

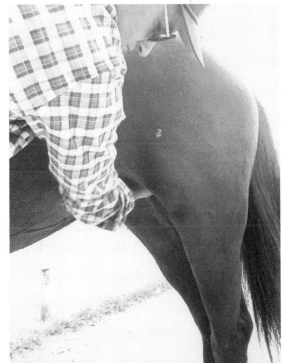

certainly suffer, too. Her level of pain or distraction may be hard for humans to measure, but only an insensitive owner could assume that she feels no pain from an internal infection.

The uterus of a mare, particularly a young one who has never foaled, is actually very resistant to infection. The vulva has strong muscles that keep contaminants out of the reproductive tract, and the uterus itself is protected by a cervix that keeps itself firmly closed except during heat. But in addition to the simple act of breeding, various circumstances can change the organ's ability to resist infection, including injury, invasion of the genital system for examination and overall poor health. Moreover, certain mares are more subject to recurring uterine infection for reasons that aren't yet clear, although research is underway into possible genetic or hormonal causes.

A veterinarian diagnoses uterine infection by doing one or more of the following: First, he or she will use a vaginal speculum to visually examine the inside of the vagina and the cervix, looking for discharge, scarring or other indications of current or former disease. Then the vet may scrape a few tissue cells from the uterus for a cytology exam. This will show if white blood cells—the mammal's infection-fighting agents—are present. Then the vet may use sterilized cotton to take a swab from the internal organs for a culture in order to identify particular pathogens. The location of the swab site depends on whether the mare is in or out of heat.

A very valuable mare may also be checked with ultrasound or other radiographic tests to see if there is fluid pooling in her uterus, another indication of infection. This is usually done with broodmares, since a fertilized embryo will not survive in a uterus filled with fluid. But a performance mare with a fluid-filled uterus will probably not perform at her highest level either, so the test might also be done on a nonbreeding animal.

Most vets are extremely careful to avoid contaminating the uterus itself during the examination. A mare's system can handle colonies of pathogens in the vagina with little ill effect, but if the same volume of germs gets into the uterus, an infection is likely to result. The vet sometimes has little choice but to invade the internal organs, since even the best ultrasound won't show which infectious agent is involved.

The visual examination is usually the most important, because symptom-free positive cultures don't necessarily mean infection. Typical uterine infection is caused by very common pathogens, including *Streptococcus*, *Pseudomonas* and *E. coli*. They may show up inside a healthy mare, although they don't usually make it to the uterus.

If there is evidence of discharge, the swab becomes particularly important, because the antibiotic will be chosen according to the pathogens present. A vet may choose not to treat the mare at all if the only sign of infection is a positive culture with no white blood cells involved.

In addition to antibiotics given either by injection or introduced into the uterus, a vet may try other procedures on resistant cases of infection. These include flushing the uterus with saline solutions, with colostrum and with solutions of the mare's own plasma plus antibiotics.

Any kind of treatment works better when the infected mare is in heat, and some vets will begin treatment of uterine infection with prostaglandin, the hormone that returns a mare to heat. There is research underway on the role of estrogens in treating uterine infection in mares, but estrogens are not yet generally approved for use in horses.

As with any other potential health problem, it's far better to prevent than to have to treat, and there are steps that a mare owner can take to lessen the chance of uterine infection. A broodmare should be bred only to a healthy stallion who is thoroughly cleaned before service.

Any sensible owner of a stud will insist that any mare to be bred by the stallion on natural cover arrive at the farm with evidence of a negative culture. In the case of artificial insemination, the stallion owner isn't so concerned about damage to his property. But for the sake of satisfied clients, breeding farms often use semen extenders that include antibiotics so that a stallion's pathogens aren't introduced into the mare.

Foaling time presents additional danger of uterine infection. It is virtually impossible to foal a mare in a sterile environment, but a foaling stall should be disinfected—and then thoroughly dried— to lessen the chance of infections being passed on by the former occupants. Anybody who helps in the foaling must wash well with a disinfectant soap or wear disposable, sterile gloves. Before delivery, the mare's external genitals and anus should be disinfected. These procedures help prevent the introduction of pathogens into the mare's reproductive tract, and also help prevent the foal from becoming infected as it travels through the birth passage.

The placenta must also be expelled by the foaling mare. It usually comes out forty-five minutes to an hour after the birth, but it can take another hour beyond that. If all of the placenta isn't out within two hours, the vet must be called (or called back). A retained placenta can cause the most serious uterine infections of all. Most mares can produce their foals without damage to either themselves or their babies, but a performance mare and her foal, being both valuable and well loved, deserve something better than their owners' trusting their health to chance.

For nonbreeding mares, attention should be paid to regular cleaning of the external genitals. Great care must be taken before inserting anything into a mare's reproductive tract, because that is the easiest way for a mare to become infected. Most vets are extremely careful about this, but if yours wants to do an internal examination of your mare without cleaning his hands thoroughly and using sterile gloves and instruments, find another vet.

Sometimes training equipment or tack can be the culprit. Tail sets used on horses who compete in events where high tail carriage is important can cause the introduction of bacteria into the genital system. If a bustle is used to relax the tail muscles, it must be carefully set and regularly cleaned so that feces aren't trapped on the device. Harness mares whose equipment includes a crupper or any other device that touches the genital region should be checked for fecal contamination and cleaned on a regular basis.

Both broodmares and maiden mares may need a Caslick's operation to prevent aspiration of air, contaminants and even feces into the internal organs. A conservative vet will perform this operation—which involves suturing the vulva—only on mares whose vulvar openings appear too large, either because of foaling or because of conformation. Others will recommend suturing every performance mare, particularly ones who gallop and are therefore more inclined to suck air into their bodies.

The Caslick's procedure not only reduces the possibility of pathogens entering the mare's genital tract, but it also lessens the possibility of a performance mare being distracted by the sound and sensation of air aspirating into her vagina. The Caslick's operation is quick and simple, although it does require some skill. The vet who performs it will have to make sure that the sutures don't cause tearing of the mare's tissues during her athletic activities. Most important, the stitches *must* be removed before a mare is bred.

Mastitis

Mastitis is a bacterial infection of the mammary glands. It's not as common in mares as it is in many other large animal species, but it does exist and can have serious consequences. Most mastitis occurs in lactating mares, but recent studies have surprised researchers by turning up a substantial amount of the disease in nonlactating and even nonpregnant mares.

A mare with even a moderate case of mastitis will be in pain. One who develops a severe case can lose udder function forever. A really severe case can lead to body-wide infection and possibly death. Mastitis in mares is not common enough to spend a lot of time worrying about, but its effects are significant enough that a quick look at the udder should be part of every mare's regular care.

A nursing mare is the most likely victim, and the owner often first notices a problem when the mare tries to prevent her foal from nursing. The next most common victim is the mare who has recently weaned her foal, and the owner usually notices the disease during a check to see if the mare is drying up properly.

But a significant portion of equine mastitis victims are not recent mothers, and some have never been bred. Owners of these mares often think at first that the horse is lame, since she may walk stiffly or favor a hind leg.

Close examination of each category of mastitis sufferer turns up a warm, swollen and painful udder, with the infected area usually limited to one of the two teats. Sometimes the flesh around the teat is also affected, with pain and swelling spreading into the flanks.

Mastitis develops when one of a number of potentially dangerous bacteria finds its way into the teat openings. A foal's mouth may cause the injury that provides the access to bacteria. In a non-lactating mare, insect bites or kick injuries may create the openings. The bacteria that cause mastitis tend to be the same ones that lead to other equine infections, and a vet will take a culture to decide which is the villain in a particular case. The disease is usually treated with antibiotics, and the choice depends on the bacteria that caused the infection. Injections of penicillin are most commonly used, but other antibiotics and combination drugs are increasingly prescribed by vets.

More is known about mastitis in cows, since the disease can cause serious financial damage to a dairy farm. A great deal of research money has been spent on finding causes and cures, and much of what has been learned about cows applies to horses. Although the development of new techniques in milking hygiene and dairy management don't apply to horses, most treatment techniques do. Cows and horses are often treated today with an antibiotic in a base infused directly into the infected teat. Hotpacks on a swollen teat will help ease a mare's discomfort as the antibiotic therapy works.

You can help prevent mastitis by keeping teats clean, handling them gently and touching them only with clean hands. Learn how your mare's teats look in their normal state, so you can seek quick veterinary help if they become infected.

10

Breeding
the Female Equine
Athlete

THE THOROUGHBRED MARE IRON MAIDEN CERTAINLY LIVED UP TO HER name. A granddaughter of Man o'War, she competed for two full seasons—a normal career for a well-bred mare. In 1945 her owner Ellwood Johnston retired her to the breeding farm, where she produced a nice filly named Iron Reward in 1946. The filly looked good from the start and even better later; among Iron Reward's offspring was 1955 Kentucky Derby winner Swaps.

But in spite of the good looks of Iron Maiden's first foal, Johnston thought there was more money to be won with her at the racetrack. There was. In 1947 Iron Maiden returned to training for two more years, winning—among other races—the Del Mar Handicap against top male horses. She retired for good with a record of sixty-one starts, most of them run after she produced a foal.

Quite an accomplishment. She not only returned to competition after foaling, but won major races. But Iron Maiden wasn't done yet. After her final retirement at the age of seven, she produced eleven more foals, including 1957 Kentucky Derby winner Iron Liege. All by herself, Iron Maiden proves that it is possible to breed a female equine athlete, and still have an athlete afterwards. But what if you don't want to take a mare out of training for two years? Do you give up the idea of breeding until her performing career is over? Not if you own a mare like May Wine.

The Standardbred mare May Wine was an ideal broodmare prospect. She was beautifully conformed and magnificently bred. Her sire, pacing Triple Crown winner Most Happy Fella, was one of the dominant sires of the breed. Her dam Maryellen Hanover was a superb producer, having previously foaled the champion pacing filly Silk Stockings. As if to prove the second generation was just as good, Silk Stockings herself had foaled world champion pacing colt Temujin. It was a family of incomparable quality, and May Wine would have been a valuable broodmare had she never set hoof on the racetrack.

But value is relative. Yes, May Wine would have been a worthwhile addition to a broodmare band even if she had raced poorly and proved that she missed out on the racing talent enjoyed by the rest of the family. She would have been worth thousands of dollars anyway, and her foals would have drawn interest at yearling auctions. But with the proof that she could really race, May Wine's value would have reached six figures rather than five, and any well-conformed offspring of hers might have brought even more.

Although May Wine had a few problems on the racetrack, she had compiled a good racing record by the time she reached the age of four. Knee problems had her in and out of training, but she accomplished a fair stakes record at the age of two and three. She had also managed a time trial in 1:55 and ⅗ seconds, respectable for a pacing mare but possibly a little slower than her pedigree promised. In 1985 there were few big-purse races available for pacing mares over the age of three, so May Wine's owners decided to breed her. A mare of her pedigree and respectable race record deserved a good stallion, so in mid-May of her four-year-old year, May Wine was bred to the legendary Niatross, at the time the richest and fastest Standardbred ever. He was the Secretariat of his sport.

As a mare in good health should, May Wine got in foal immediately, but her handlers quickly realized that her good health went beyond her ability to conceive. Her knee problems were cured and she finally had the soundness and ability to concentrate to accomplish what her pedigree had always suggested she might—a major stakes win and a truly fast race record.

So, in spite of the fact that she was carrying a foal by a stallion whose stud fee was $40,000, May Wine was kept in training to try for that fast race record. She got it and then some.

Three and a half months after becoming in foal to Niatross, May Wine paced a mile at the Meadowlands in 1:52 and ⅗ seconds, a world record time for a Standardbred mare. The fetus, who probably set some kind of a record, too, developed into a healthy filly foaled the following spring.

Most people don't own a mare worth hundreds of thousands of dollars as a performer, or one carrying a fetus likely to be worth even more at a future auction. Still, most owners of performance mares tend to think they must do one thing or the other with their animals—either breed them or use them. They're convinced that the two activities can't be combined, at least for the eleven months of the pregnancy and the five or six months before weaning. Most people also believe that, while a mare may obviously be used after foaling, she will never again compete at the level she did before her pregnancy.

Evidence, both from observation and research, suggests otherwise. Unless foaling causes physical damage, recurrent uterine infection or other problems resulting from the trauma of birth, there is no reason a mare can't regain her physical condition or form.

As for her mental form, that depends. Pregnancy can change a mare's personality. Sometimes that's good, since even one pregnancy—carried to term or not—can cause an erratic mare to have regular, consistent cycles that will continue through her life. Many trainers and riders report that mares become mellower and less inclined to waste energy after a pregnancy, and many concentrate better on their training.

But sometimes the changes, although pleasant, aren't conducive to good performance. A mare can be too mellow for her sport. There's another problem with returning a mare to training after a pregnancy. If her sport is one in which youth counts, the loss of a year or two of training may hurt her chances of success. So the possibility of reducing the time away from training becomes intriguing.

Just how dangerous is it to use an in-foal mare for anything more strenuous than casual riding or driving? Some conservative experts say it's dangerous enough not to try it. They point out that mares don't have particularly good live-foal rates anyway, and they believe that no wanted pregnancy should be subjected to unnecessary risk. The equine embryo does not attach to the uterine lining until about fifty days into gestation, and opponents of heavy exercise for the pregnant mare feel the embryo might be subjected to undue stress by bouncing around.

But other experts point out that wild mares continue their normal activities of moving around to graze and running away from predators right up to the moment of foaling. Historians tell us that working mares of the past continued their work until the girth or harness couldn't be buckled around them. Everybody had to earn a living in the old days.

As for the effects on performance, equine physiologists tell us that fetus growth is so slight during the first few months of pregnancy that most mare owners can expect—in terms of physical performance—essentially the same results from an in-foal mare that they got from her before she conceived. She probably won't get any better, unless she is another May Wine, but there is no physical reason for her abilities to decline.

This chapter is not intended to be a definitive guide to the care and management of a broodmare, but concentrates rather on her pregnancy as it relates to her other activities. Remember to consult your veterinarian before making a final decision about breeding a mare whose real job is performance. In the meantime, here are some of the points you should consider before making your decision.

Most mares can work several months into their pregnancies.

Dr. Katrin Hinrichs believes that, during the early months of pregnancy, mares behave and perform pretty much as they do while not in foal.

When Does Pregnancy Become a Burden?

You have at least four months of normal physical shape and size, followed by another four months of a light change in your mare's physique before pregnancy becomes a burden to her.

"The real growth is in the last third, and mostly the last two months of gestation," says Dr. Katrin Hinrichs, director of the Equine Reproduction Center at Tufts New England Veterinary Medical Center. "Up to that point, the foal is growing, but it's not so big that it's going to be a burden for the mare to carry around."

In fact, the weight of the fetus is negligible compared to the overall weight of the mare, at least during the first few months of gestation. According to statistics, a normal mare's three-month-old fetus will be only 5 inches from the poll to the root of the tail and weigh only about 5 ounces. After four months, it will have grown to 9 inches and weigh less than 2 pounds. Even after six months, the embryo will be less than 2 feet long and weigh 10 or 11 pounds. That means that a normal-sized sporting mare will be carrying a six-month fetus that's only about 1 percent of her body weight. The placenta and other weight gain would add a little more, but it's obvious that a six-month pregnancy does not have a great deal of effect on a mare's mobility.

Seven months after conception, a foal averages 18 to 22 pounds, and at eight months 26 to 40 pounds. After eight months, growth is much more rapid. The weight of the fetus will increase by as much as 20 pounds in each of the three months prior to birth.

Particularly with a toned maiden mare, a pregnancy of less than six, seven or even eight months is usually not discernible. But there are other effects of pregnancy. "The mare is obviously going to be under a little different hormonal stimulation," Dr. Hinrichs says, "but in a horse we don't see the hormonal effects that we see in people. Nobody has noticed that there's a decrease in desire to exercise in early pregnancy, for example." As the owner and trainer of May Wine discovered, pregnant mares may even become more enthusiastic about their work.

Pregnancy Loss and the Working Mare

If you have made a careful decision to breed—and if you have paid a hefty stud fee—you are certainly going to be concerned about more than your mare's athletic performance. Once your mare has conceived, you have a second horse to worry about. Nearly everyone agrees that some exercise benefits mare and embryo. Pregnancy-related colic and circulatory problems are less common in mares who exercise, and working mares are less likely to suffer diseases caused by too much food and too little exercise.

Still, there's a big difference between the kind of exercise a mare gets by strolling around a paddock and the kind she gets carrying a rider over jumps or around a racecourse. Early embryonic loss strikes mares whatever their equine way of life. What we want to know is this: Is it more likely to strike the working mare than the mare who takes it easy for eleven months? Stress, illness and uterine infections have been implicated in pregnancy loss. Researchers have looked at each to try to determine its role in embryonic loss and the likelihood of particular mares being affected.

Stress

Although stress can be a culprit in equine abortion, the kind of stress caused by work does not appear to be a factor. A study conducted in Germany involved having helicopters buzz tied mares; another—probably more sensible—done at Colorado State University involved vanning pregnant mares during hormonally vulnerable periods of early pregnancy. In neither case did the stress affect the course of the pregnancy.

Dr. Hinrichs says, "It's been fairly well shown that there's little possibility that stress—such as a mare's falling down when she's jumping, or that kind of thing—can cause abortion in the horse. It doesn't seem to be something to worry about."

Illness

The kind of stress that does bring about unwanted abortion is more likely to be the result of illness, to which working and nonworking pregnant mares are usually equally vulnerable. Performance mares, however, are more likely to be exposed to other horses, since stabling and shipping ensure that. Therefore the working mare is more likely to be exposed to a virus or bacteria that can cause an abortion-inducing illness.

Simple rhinopneumonitis—a cold—can increase the risk of abortion in a pregnant mare. Her condition does not make her more or less likely to get the disease than a nonpregnant mare, but it's the contact with other horses that makes her more vulnerable. Unfortunately, while other horses get the sniffles, a pregnant mare who catches the virus may abort.

Housing for a pregnant working mare should be planned and arranged with her condition in mind. She should have as little direct contact as possible with other horses likely to have colds, particularly young horses during the fall and early winter, when almost all of them seem to come down with viruses. Any young or not-so-young horse with a cough or discharge from eyes or nose should be kept as far away as is feasible.

A vaccine against equine viral rhinopneumonitis—the disease that causes a great many virus-induced abortions—is now available. It's sold under the name Pneumabort-K and has proven about 80 percent effective. The manufacturer, Fort Dodge, recommends doses in the fifth, seventh and ninth months of pregnancy. Nonbreeding mares and other horses may also be vaccinated, although the disease is not as dangerous to them as it is to fetuses. Other vaccinations are important for pregnant mares, whether or not they are exposed to a large number of new horses. Consult your veterinarian or county agent for recommendations for your region.

Uterine Infection

Bacterial infection of the uterus can also cause abortion, but working in-foal mares are usually no more subject to uterine infection than any other pregnant mares. The actual process of getting a mare in foal is what endangers the pregnant mare, working or otherwise. Bacterial infection in the uterus can be caused by bacteria introduction during breeding, during internal examination or during foaling itself. The bacterial problem can remain from one foaling to the next. None of these possibilities is related to the work the mare does.

But there is one situation in which a performing or other kind of working mare is more likely to become infected. "A racehorse who's very low in weight might not have enough fat around the vulvar lips to keep them very well closed," Dr. Hinrichs says. "When they're running they can aspirate air into the vagina. In rare cases that can lead to problems."

A few mares have poor vulvar conformation, consequently air and debris can be sucked into the vagina during even moderate work. If bacteria enter as well, they may reach and infect the uterus. This is a problem in a nonpregnant mare, but it can be a disaster in a pregnant one. Caslick's procedure is often done on nonpregnant windsuckers, and it should certainly be done on pregnant ones.

Many big breeding farms routinely suture in-foal mares, regardless of their level of exercise or the conformation of their external genitals. Any breeder who does this *must* keep a careful eye on the mare in order to remove the sutures before foaling. Otherwise, the vulva can be badly torn during the delivery process.

Injury

Injury, particularly injury that causes infection, may be more common in a working mare, although even mares in paddocks can injure themselves and each other. A serious injury may be stressful enough to affect a fetus, although most owners of injured mares will be concerned first about the survival of their mares and only secondarily about the fetus. Infection introduced into a mare by an injury is a potential danger to a fetus even if the initial injury was not serious, so any cut or scrape should be quickly treated. Any medication stronger than a common antiseptic should be cleared with the mare's veterinarian before use on a pregnant mare.

Drugs

There's one additional topic to consider before doing serious training or performance work with a pregnant mare. A study completed at Washington State University showed that the common analgesic phenylbutazone—used on many racing and performance horses—crossed the placental barrier in mares given regular doses. The fetus and the amniotic fluid showed significant—possibly toxic—concentrations of the drug. Those who conducted the study don't believe occasional doses of bute would have that effect.

The study was extremely limited and more research on the subject is likely to be done, but in the meantime it would be wise to avoid using regular bute on a pregnant mare. A cautious owner might want to skip bute altogether during the eleven months of gestation.

Other medications and chemicals should be used with care during pregnancy as well, because many of them have never been adequately studied for their potential toxic effect on fetuses. Something as seemingly simple as a chemical leg brace might get into a mare's system and cross the placental barrier into the foal.

Steroids

Various kinds of steroids are also used on many performance and racing horses. The corticosteroids are used to treat joint inflammations; the anabolic steroids are supposed to improve muscle mass and appetite. The corticosteroids are often injected directly into inflamed ankles or knees. Little research has been done on their effects on pregnancy, but research on performance horses suggests that overuse can lead to degenerative joint disease, adrenal gland failure and laminitis. The latter is particularly important to owners of pregnant mares, since their increasing weight sometimes makes them more vulnerable to that deadly and crippling disease anyway. If your mare is so sore that she needs corticosteroids to perform, she's not healthy enough for you to consider working and breeding her at the same time.

The second category of steroids consists of the anabolic variety, used to increase muscle mass and aggression in racing and performance horses. Plenty of research exists on their effects on equine reproduction. If your mare is currently receiving anabolic steroids, you may not have to decide whether or not to stop them during her pregnancy. It's possible she'll be unable to get in foal at all. (See Chapter 2 for information on anabolic steroids and reproduction.)

Nutrition

Among the misconceptions about equine nutrition is the belief that performance horses and pregnant mares need substantially more and significantly different food from other horses. A pregnant mare who is still performing becomes a likely candidate for being fed enormous quantities of high-protein, high-energy and high-caloric feed. The result may be an overweight mare who can't work well early in her pregnancy, has trouble late in gestation and who may pass on the diseases of overnutrition to her offspring. Pregnant mares do need more feed than nonpregnant ones, but they don't need it until quite late in their pregnancies, when they are probably taking it easy anyway.

For the first eight months of gestation, mares should be fed as they were before pregnancy—according to the level of their activity. Active horses do need more feed than inactive ones, but what they need is more calories rather than a higher percentage of protein or vitamins or anything else. Adult horses need at least 9 percent

During early pregnancy, the nutritional requirements of mares don't differ from those of stallions, geldings and nonpregnant mares of similar size and use. (Photo credit: Mark Morelli/Tufts University)

protein in their diets, regardless of their level of activity. Feeding a higher percentage does not appear to be a danger, unless the percentage is increased drastically.

According to the National Research Council, which releases nutritional guidelines for both humans and domestic animals, a 900-pound inactive horse needs about 14,000 calories a day. A moderately active one needs about 24,000. The active one will get more protein, but not a higher percentage in terms of the total diet.

An in-foal mare needs both more calories and a higher percentage of protein, as well as increased levels of certain vitamins, calcium and phosphorus. But these increased levels are only moderate—a minimum 11.5 percent protein rather than 9; 15,000 calories rather than 14,000 for an inactive mare. Moreover, these increased requirements come only during the last three months of gestation. Most of the specialized feeds designed for pregnant mares contain more than enough protein, vitamins and minerals for a pregnant mare, and it's rarely necessary to supplement them.

So here are the general guidelines for your pregnant working mare: (1) For the first eight months, continue feeding her the ration for a horse at her activity level (assuming you've been buying and feeding a well-balanced feed); (2) for the final three months, give her substantially more protein and vitamins and a few more calories, even though she'll probably not be working much; (3) ask your vet's advice in choosing feed and supplements for the pregnant mare, or try one of the national brands balanced for broodmares; (4) watch the quantities and watch to see that her ribs don't disappear in a pillow of fat that can't be explained away by the growing fetus.

The Nursing Mare

After foaling, you'll lose the use of your mare for a while. But if her normal use is light riding at home, you won't have to do without her for long. A foal is running around within a day or two, and the mare's uterus is back to its normal position within a week or two. She could possibly be ridden then, with her foal trotting alongside, for brief periods. She shouldn't be ridden too far from her barn or home paddock, because foals need to eat and rest often.

Lactating mares also need to eat and rest often, and they need to eat much more than pregnant mares. Milk production requires an enormous amount of energy, particularly during the first three months of lactation. That 900-pound mare who needed only 15,000 calories a day during late pregnancy will need more than 24,000 while nursing. The calorie figure goes up if she's getting extra exercise. Instead of 11.5 percent protein in her diet, she'll need 13.3, and her calcium and phosphorus requirements will nearly double. She will need specialized feed, but only during the period she is actually nursing her foal. At weaning, it's back to regular feed for her.

When to Wean

Weaning means your mare can return to her regular activities as well as her regular feed, so anybody who owns a performance or pleasure mare often counts the days until she can be separated from her foal. Still, nobody wants to be cruel to either mother or foal, and nobody wants to cause physical or mental damage to the foal by weaning too early.

Left to nature, weaning is likely to occur any time after six months. Mare and foal usually begin drifting apart late in the foal's first year, and they've separated completely by the time the mare has her next foal eleven or twelve months after the birth of the first.

But weaning is rarely left to nature. Professional breeders usually wean at four to five months. Some small operations will leave mares and foals together until the foal is six months old or even older. You can bet that Secretariat, Jet Run, Man o'War, Citation, Niatross, Touch of Class and other products of a professional breeding operation were weaned at four to five months.

Breeders find that age a good compromise for the foal. He's small enough to handle during the difficult process of weaning, but big enough to be able to eat feed, hay and grass. He's young enough that he hasn't yet started to play too roughly with his dam—and risk receiving a crippling or even fatal kick. And he's old enough to readjust his orientation from his dam to other weanlings or to people. So four to five months is a good age for weaning, and after four or five months you look forward to having the use of your mare again.

You can't wait that long? You want to know if you can wean earlier without damaging either mare or foal? Yes, if you proceed with caution. Foals begin eating solid foods by the time they're a month old, and by two months they can live without their dam's milk. Some professional breeders do wean at two months, and they report no serious problems because of it. Some even wean on a regular basis as early as five or six weeks.

The only candidate for early weaning is a good eating, healthy foal who is growing and developing normally. He must be familiar with and be willing to eat his future food *before* he's separated from his dam. Some breeders find that, after early weaning, they have to give a milk-based pelleted food like Calf Manna to encourage the foal to make the transition from a mother's milk diet to a horse-feed diet.

Mares weaned from their foals early are neither more nor less likely to develop mastitis, which often appears a week or two after weaning. Among the signs: heat and swelling in the udder or, in a working mare, lameness in the side where the mastitis has occurred. Call the vet to have your mare treated as soon as you see signs that she's infected.

Separation at Birth

Many fine and successful horses have been taken from their dams at birth and have shown no ill effects as a result. It's hardly recommended, but it can be done if circumstances warrant. The procedure, which usually involves the use of nurse mares, is almost commonplace on some large farms.

Geography can play a role. When breed registries require that

This seven-week-old filly is eating on her own and could survive nicely apart from her dam. She'll probably stay with the mare until a more usual weaning age, but if the mare has to go back to work, both should survive early weaning with few problems.

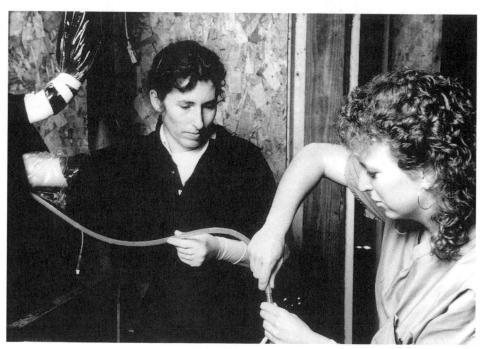

Dr. Katrin Hinrichs (left) and Tufts technician Karen Swain flush embryos from a donor mare. (Photo credit: Tufts University)

stallion and mare be on the same farm at the time of conception—this includes the racing breeds—owners are often faced with the dilemma of trying to protect a young foal from the stress of traveling while getting its dam bred to a distant stallion. During the years that the great Northern Dancer was at stud in Maryland, the foals of his Kentucky-based mares were often placed on nurse mares so their dams could be vanned to Maryland to be bred. As a result, classic winners and champions by the dozen have been raised by nurse mares.

The death of the dam while foaling or shortly after, her rejection of the foal or her inability to produce milk will also create a need for a nurse mare. A large draft-type mare is the most likely candidate to raise somebody else's foal, but other breeds are also used. The coldblooded mares tend to be good milkers, as well as most willing to accept a strange foal with minimal odor-masking.

Owners lacking access to a nurse mare can raise a foal by hand using commercial milk replacers. It's a time-consuming process, and foals are undoubtedly best raised by members of their own species. But many people have raised useful horses by hand, although it's generally not something you would choose to do just to get the use of a mare a few months earlier.

The Nonpregnant Dam—Embryo Transfer

If the use of your mare is so important to you that you don't want to take any time out for her pregnancy and foal-raising, if you want to be on the cutting edge of equine reproduction technology, if you have a lot of money—then maybe embryo transfer is for the two of you. If she's a Thoroughbred race mare, forget it. The Jockey Club will not register the foal. But if the foal is destined for an activity where breed doesn't matter, such as show jumping or dressage, or if it's a member of a breed that permits the process, such as Quarter Horse, Tennessee Walking Horse or Saddlebred, here are the facts.

At ovulation the mare is bred, usually by artificial insemination.

A week later, after the egg has been fertilized and has traveled through the oviduct to the uterus, the microscopic embryo is flushed from the uterus into a collecting vessel. The mare then goes home to race, jump, perform—whatever work she normally does.

The embryo is inserted into a recipient mare, usually a healthy, phlegmatic, mixed-breed animal, who then carries the foal to term. The foal is raised by the recipient mare. At first, the entire procedure was done at the handful of equine medical centers that offer the process. Now it's possible for local veterinarians to flush the embryo from a valuable mare and ship just the embryo to a center that implants and then certifies the recipient mare as in foal. The recipient then goes to whoever is going to own her foal. The American Quarter Horse Association, which maintains the most complete statistics on the process, estimates the current average cost of an embryo transfer procedure to be $3,500. That doesn't include stud fee, shipping and post-conception care. The figure may go down as the process becomes more common, or it may increase, as most medical expenses tend to do.

The evidence is not yet in on whether embryo-transfer foals perform differently from naturally borne foals. Not until there are literally thousands of embryo foals performing in sports where good records are kept will we be able to draw conclusions. Quarter Horse racing allows and keeps track of embryo performers, and AQHA statistics show that the percentage of top performers among embryo horses is higher than the percentage of top performers in the breed as a whole. We can't draw meaningful conclusions from that, since only mares of high quality will be used to produce embryos for transfer, and that alone should ensure that embryo foals are better than the average Quarter Horse.

There is another area of interest and concern to scientists. It's possible that the surrogate mother has a long-term physical effect on the foal, even though the foal carries no genes from her. All studies so far seem to show the same initial effect of the surrogate, indicating that a foal from small natural parents carried by a large mare will be larger at birth than it would have been if carried by the real mother. And while a study Colorado State University conducted during the early 1980s suggests that the foals eventually mature according to their genetic characteristics, and that the influence of the surrogate disappears, more recent study at the Academy of Agriculture at Krakow, Poland, conducted between 1984 and 1990, suggests something else altogether.

In this study, several pairs of sex-matched full siblings, one of each carried by the natural pony mother and one by a large draft-mare mother, showed initial findings similar to those of the Colorado State study. The offspring of big mares were larger at birth and during foalhood than their siblings. But the difference was still noticeable at the age of five, when the offspring were adults.

A University of North Carolina study that involved mice rather than horses showed even more dramatic effects of surrogacy. In the study, reported in 1990, researchers conducted three years of inbreeding through two hundred generations of mice to produce a group of genetically identical big mice and another group of smaller mice.

The scientists transferred embryos from both the large mouse and the small mouse pool into females from both size groups. In almost every case, the large females bore bigger and differently conformed fetuses than the small females, regardless of which group the embryo came from. The size differences, as well as differences in bone structure, internal organs and general health remained through the lives of the young mice. It was obvious to the North Carolina scientists that surrogate mothers affect their fetuses—at least in the mouse world—in measurable ways, even though they share no common genes.

Such information brings up an ethical dilemma of embryo transfer in breeds where horses are sold according to their pedigrees: How does a buyer figure in the effects of the surrogate? And there's a practical dilemma, too. If your agile jumping mare's embryo is implanted into a Percheron, do you get a bigger, stronger but still agile jumper? Or do you get a big animal who jumps like a Percheron? Only research and experience will tell.

What you *do* get is a mare who can continue to work after conceiving a foal—one who can be setting records, earning money and winning acclaim while she might have been waddling around a paddock awaiting the birth of her foal. Take Dash For Speed, one of the great Quarter racing mares in history. In the spring of 1990, the millionaire and All-American Gold Cup winner was bred to the stallion Streakin' Six. Her embryo was transferred to another mare and she was returned to training.

In her first start a couple of months later, she set a track record at Los Alamitos in California. In December, when she would have been eight months pregnant, she won $125,000 in the Champion of Champions race, Quarter Horse racing's most celebrated event for older horses. Five stallions and geldings and five mares finished behind her. Altogether, Dash For Speed won $209,000 after being bred. Being able to race long after her foal was conceived gave her a new record for the breed—a total of ten Grade One wins in her career.

Not every mare is worth the time and expense of embryo transfer, either in terms of her work potential or the value of her genes. But it's a technique likely to be increasingly common among top female performers in the various horse sports.

Truly valuable mares may eventually be involved in a process even more elaborate. Experiments are underway in Europe and the United States for *in vitro* fertilization of the mare. In this process the donor mare—the one whose genes are so desirable that you want to pass them on—would not even have to conceive. Her matured eggs would be removed, fertilized in a test tube, and then placed in a recipient mare. The process would be ideal for a mare who can ovulate but who cannot carry a foal to term. Unfortunately, the horse is resistant to this process as well as to superovulation, which would allow the harvest of numerous eggs each month from an individual donor. But there is another potential method—*in vivo* fertilization.

Dr. Hinrichs has succeeded at Tufts in transferring oocytes—eggs not yet matured for ovulation—from donors to recipients, then maturing and fertilizing them in the recipient mares. The process is still highly experimental, but its implications for valuable performance mares are clear. A mare who simply cannot conceive, or one who dies young, could still pass on her genes.

The process is not yet available outside the laboratory. Even if it were, the reactions of many breed registries—particularly the powerful Jockey Club—might not be favorable. Moreover, the cost is likely to be quite high. But who could put a price on oocytes from the $7-million broodmare Miss Oceana, who died in Kentucky producing only her second foal, or the great hurdler Dawn Run, who broke her neck in a steeplechase in France, or Ruffian, dead at the age of three in a barn in New York? No medical procedure could cost a fraction of what one of those unfertilized eggs would be worth.

As for other mares—remember May Wine. Even without re-sorting to the most expensive procedures in veterinary science, a mare can be in foal and can perform for at least half of her preg-nancy. She can then resume performing again a couple of months after foaling. And if you want to know if she can perform as well when she returns to training, think of Iron Maiden. A mare might just be able to produce the dam of a Kentucky Derby winner, return to action and win the biggest event of her life, then go back to the breeding shed and produce her own Derby winner. It has been done.

Recommended Reading

IN TERMS OF HEALTH CARE AND BASIC HANDLING MALE AND FEMALE horses are more alike than they are different. A good book that covers the principles of health, nutrition, training or handling will be equally useful to owners of mares, geldings or stallions. Some books are a little more useful to mare owners, either because they include information specific to the female horse or because they cover situations more common to mares than male horses. Here are some of my favorites. Most are still in print. Those out-of-print books can often be found in horse book catalogs and in secondhand book stores. If not, check your local library.

Breeding

Lose, M. Phyllis. *Blessed Are the Broodmares*. 2d ed. Howell Book House, 1991. Dr. Lose is not a great believer in using pregnant mares, but her book is as good as you'll find on the subject of mares and breeding. She loves mares, and it shows.

General Care and Handling

Price, Steven, ed. *The Whole Horse Catalog*. Fireside, 1985. Price and various experts offer a taste of almost every aspect of the horse world. It's a good basic book to have around the barn.

Stoneridge, M. A. *A Horse of Your Own: The Rider-Owner's Complete Guide*. 4th ed. Doubleday, 1990. This classic provides most of the basic information you need for day-to-day care of horses of either sex.

Grooming

Harris, Susan. *Grooming to Win*. 2d ed. Howell Book House, 1991. Offers suggestions on how to maximize good points and minimize flaws. Emphasizes good nutrition and conditioning.

Strickland, Charlene. *Show Grooming: The Look of a Winner*. Breakthrough, 1986. An all-breeds, all-event collection of tips, several of which are particularly appropriate to mares.

Horse Health

Giffen, James, and Tom Gore. *Horse Owner's Veterinary Handbook*. Howell Book House, 1989. Up-to-date, complete and well indexed.

Hayes, M. Horace. *Veterinary Notes for Horse Owners*. 17th ed. Prentice Hall Press, 1988. The classic veterinary text for owners has been used by decades of horsepeople.

Nutrition

Hintz, Harold F. *Horse Nutrition: A Practical Guide*. Prentice Hall Press, 1983. Intended for the layperson, it is readable and thorough.

National Research Council. *Nutrient Requirements of Domestic Animals*. National Academy Press, 1989. This is not nearly so readable, but it represents the best and latest research. Copies are available through the National Academy Press, 2101 Constitution Avenue, NW, Washington, DC 20418. It costs $17.95.

Sources

MOST TACK SHOPS AND GENERAL-INTEREST BOOKSTORES HAVE AT LEAST a modest selection of horse books, but to get some of the suggested books—and to see what else is coming out—you need a specialized source. Here are some suggestions:

Dover Saddlery. Box 5837, Holliston, MA 01746. Their tack and equipment catalog includes dozens of good, current titles with accurate descriptions.

Equine Research Inc. P.O. Box 5547, Grand Prairie, TX 75053. They publish primarily for professional horsepeople, concentrating on health, breeding and race training. While expensive, their books are as thorough as you'll find anywhere.

Knight Equestrian Books. P.O. Box 78, Boothbay, ME 04556.

Miller's. P.O. Box 883, Rutherford, N.J. 07070-0883. This mail-order tack and riding apparel company includes books in several of its specialized catalogs.

J. A. Allen. 1 Lower Grosvenor Place, Buckingham Palace Road, London, England SW1W 0EL. The single best source of horse books in the world. Write for their catalog. Shipping isn't that expensive and they take credit cards.

Pegasos Press. 535 Cordova Road #163, Santa Fe, NM 87501-4143. Call 1-800-537-8558 for a catalog. Very complete and very efficient. Not quite J. A. Allen, but not bad.

Robin Bledsoe, Bookseller. 1640-BD Massachusetts Avenue, Cambridge, MA 02138. New, used and antique equestrian titles.

State Line Tack. Route 121, P.O. Box 1217, Plaistow, NH 03865-1217. This discount tack catalog usually includes five or six pages of current books, and best of all—they discount book prices, too!

Bibliography

Books

Akers, Dwight. *Drivers Up*. Putnam's, 1938.

Alexander, David. *History and Romance of the Horse*. Cooper Square Publishers, 1963.

Billard, Jules, ed. *World of the American Indian*. National Geographic Society, 1974.

Bolus, Jim, ed. *Derby 115*. Magazine Art, Ltd., 1989.

Brander, Michael. *Complete Guide to Horsemanship*. A and C Black, 1985.

Churchill, Peter. *Practical Showjumping*. Howell Book House, 1990.

Clayton, Michael, and William C. Steinkraus. *Complete Book of Show Jumping*. Crown, 1975.

Compton, Lynn. *Training and Showing the Cutting Horse*. Prentice Hall Press, 1990.

Daily Racing Form. *American Racing Manual*. Daily Racing Form, 1991.

Denhardt, Robert. *Quarter Horse: A Story of Two Centuries*. University of Oklahoma Press, 1967.

Dunning, Al. *Reining*. Western Horseman, 1983.

Fraser, Clarence, ed. *Merck Veterinary Manual*. Merck & Co., 1991.

Gianoli, Luigi. *Horses and Horsemanship Through the Ages*. Crown, 1969.

Goeldner, Christian T. *The Thoroughbred Field Hunter*. A. S. Barnes, 1977.

Green, Ben K. *Horse Conformation*. Northland Press, 1969.

Haines, Francis. *Horses in America.* Thomas Y. Crowell, 1971.

Harris, H. A. *Sport in Greece and Rome.* Cornell University Press, 1972.

Kaplan, Janice. *Women and Sports.* Viking, 1979.

Kays, John M. *The Horse,* 2d ed. Arco, 1982.

Kidd, Jane. *Festival of Dressage.* Arco, 1982.

———. *Practical Dressage.* Howell Book House, 1990.

———. *The Better Horse.* Arco, 1984.

Laune, Paul. *America's Quarter Horses.* Doubleday, 1973.

Mayo, Jane, and Bob Gray. *Championship Barrel Racing.* Cordovan Corporation, 1967.

Miller, Robert W. *Imprint Training of the Newborn Foal.* Western Horseman, 1991.

———. *Western Horse Behavior and Training.* Doubleday, 1975.

Morris, Desmond. *Horsewatching.* Crown, 1988.

Pawlak, John, ed. *Trotting and Pacing Guide.* United States Trotting Association, 1991.

Podhajsky, Alois. *My Horses, My Teachers.* Doubleday, 1968.

Rees, Lucy. *The Horse's Mind.* Prentice Hall Press, 1985.

Rooney, James R. *The Lame Horse.* A. S. Barnes, 1974.

Ryder, Tom. *The High Stepper.* J. A. Allen, 1979.

Sautter, Frederic J., and John A. Glover. *Behavior, Development, and Training of the Horse.* Arco, 1981.

Smith, Bradley. *The Horse in the West.* Leon Amiel, 1969.

Smythe, R. H. *The Mind of the Horse.* Stephen Greene Press, 1965.

Steinkraus, William C. *Reflections on Riding and Jumping.* Doubleday, 1991.

———. *Riding and Jumping.* Doubleday, 1961.

Stoneridge, M. A. *Great Horses of Our Time.* Doubleday, 1972.

Strassburger, John, ed. *American Horses in Sport 1991.* Chronicle of the Horse, 1992.

Swenson, M. J., ed. *Duke's Physiology of Domestic Animals.* Cornell University Press, 1977.

Taylor, Louis. *Ride Western.* Harper and Row, 1968.

Van Gelder, Richard G. *Biology of Mammals.* Scribner's, 1969.

Vernam, Glenn R. *Man on Horseback.* Harper and Row, 1964.

Vernon, Arthur. *History and Romance of the Horse.* Dover, 1946.

Willoughby, D. P. *Growth and Nutrition of the Horse.* A. S. Barnes, 1975.

Periodicals

Beckman, Bruce. "Embryo Transfer—You Be the Judge." *Quarter Racing Journal*, April 1990.

Biles, Deirdre. "The Practice of Gelding." *Blood-Horse*, October 24, 1987.

———. "Seeking a Perfect Production Record." *Blood-Horse*, December 30, 1989.

De Koning, Rick. "The Mating Game." *Blood-Horse*, July 29, 1989.

Donovan, K. T. "Repairing a Deficiency." *Blood-Horse*, February 9, 1991.

Eddy, Vera. "Racing for Two." *Hoofbeats*, March 1985.

Henneke, Don R. "Reproductive Anatomy and Physiology of the Mare." *Quarter Racing Journal*, January 1989.

Herbert, Kimberly. "A Time for Preparation." *Blood-Horse*, December 24, 1988.

———. "Battle of the Breeding Season." *Blood-Horse*, November 23, 1991.

———. "Utilizing Teasers." *Blood-Horse*, January 12, 1991.

Hintz, H. F., R. L. Hintz, and L. D. Van Vleck. "Growth Rate of Thoroughbreds. Effect of Age of Dam, Year and Month of Birth, and Sex of Foal." *Journal of Animal Science*, vol. 48, no. 3, 1979.

Hoffman, Dean. "Can Peace Corps Beat the Boys?" *Hoofbeats*, May 1989.

———. "Easy Does It." *Hoofbeats*, April 1991.

"Interpreting Animals' Vocal Messages." *Animal Health Newsletter*, Cornell University School of Veterinary Medicine, October 1989.

Jager, Nita. "Steroid-Induced Skeletal Disease in Horses." *Backstretch*, July 1984.

Jones, William. "Factors Affecting Racing Ability." *Horseman's Journal*, April 1984.

———. "Muscular Causes of Poor Performance." *Quarter Racing Journal*, October 1990.

Kilby, Emily. "Manipulated Motherhood." *Equus*, December 1982.

Lenz, Thomas R. "Care of the Pregnant and Foaling Mare." *Quarter Racing Journal*, January 1992.

———. "Equine Castration." *Quarter Racing Journal*, September 1991.

———. "Equine Dentistry." *Quarter Racing Journal*, October 1991.

———. "Steroids: Their Use and Misuse in the Horse." *Quarter Racing Journal*, June 1991.

Ott, Emiline. "Virginia's Gold Cup." *Spur*, May–June 1987.

Pagan, Joe D. "The Feeding of the Horse." *Blood-Horse*, May 27, 1989.

Potter, John T. "Nutritional Management of the Broodmare." *Quarter Racing Journal*, December 1989.

"Safe and Rational Approach to Feeding Horses." *Animal Health Newsletter*, Cornell University School of Veterinary Medicine, March 1991.

Sellnow, Les. "Steroids—Use in the Breeding Animal." *Blood-Horse*, March 21, 1987.

———. "When Is a Dam Not a Dam?" *Blood-Horse*, September 1, 1990.

———. and Deirdre Biles. "Steroids." *Blood-Horse*, July 28, 1990.

Thomas, Heather Smith. "Mastitis Can Be Serious in Horses." *Chronicle of the Horse*, January 3, 1992.

Tower, Whitney. "Fillies vs. Colts—An Appraisal." *Classic*, June–July 1976.

Tyznik, W. J. "About Feeding Horses." *Hoofbeats*, May 1986.

Weeks, Helma, ed. "The Effects of Anabolic Steroids on Mare Behavior." *Bellwether*, Summer 1986.

"Why Some Mares Are More Susceptible to Uterine Infection." *Animal Health Newsletter*, Cornell University School of Veterinary Medicine, March 1992.

Williams, Rhonda. "The Sorrow of Victory." *Blood-Horse*, November 3, 1990.

Worrall, Margaret. "Much More Than a Touch of Class." *Maryland Horse*, September 1984.

Index